A GIFT FOR:

_____

FROM:

_____

DATE:

_____

RESILIENT
HOPE

100 Devotions for Building Endurance
in an Unpredictable World

CHRISTINE CAINE

THOMAS NELSON
Since 1798

Published in Nashville, Tennessee, by Thomas Nelson. Thomas Nelson is a registered trademark of HarperCollins Christian Publishing, Inc.

Published in association with Yates & Yates, www.yates2.com.

Thomas Nelson titles may be purchased in bulk for educational, business, fundraising, or sales promotional use. For information, please email SpecialMarkets@ThomasNelson.com.

Unless otherwise noted, Scripture quotations are from the Christian Standard Bible®. Copyright © 2017 by Holman Bible Publishers. Used by permission. Christian Standard Bible® and CSB® are federally registered trademarks of Holman Bible Publishers, all rights reserved.

Scripture quotations marked AMP are from the Amplified® Bible (AMP). Copyright © 2015 by The Lockman Foundation. Used by permission. www.Lockman.org

Scripture quotations marked ESV are from the ESV ® Bible (The Holy Bible, English Standard Version®). Copyright © 2001 by Crossway, a publishing ministry of Good News Publishers. Used by permission. All rights reserved.

Scripture quotations marked NIV are from the Holy Bible, New International Version®, NIV® Copyright © 1973, 1978, 1984, 2011 by Biblica, Inc.® Used by permission of Zondervan. All rights reserved worldwide. www.zondervan.com. The "NIV" and "New International Version" are trademarks registered in the United States Patent and Trademark Office by Biblica, Inc.®

Scripture quotations marked NRSV are from the New Revised Standard Version Bible, copyright © 1989 National Council of the Churches of Christ in the United States of America. Used by permission. All rights reserved.

Any Internet addresses, phone numbers, or company or product information printed in this book are offered as a resource and are not intended in any way to be or to imply an endorsement by Thomas Nelson, nor does Thomas Nelson vouch for the existence, content, or services of these sites, phone numbers, companies, or products beyond the life of this book.

ISBN 978-0-310-45760-2 (audiobook)
ISBN 978-0-310-45797-8 (eBook)
ISBN 978-0-310-45796-1 (HC)

Printed in China
22 23 24 25 26 GRI 10 9 8 7 6 5 4 3 2 1

To my dear friend Dawn Jackson.
Your passion for hiking opened up a whole new world for me.

CONTENTS

INTRODUCTION

There are few sporting events that can bring me to my feet, move me to tears, and fill my heart with equal parts of joy and sorrow like the Olympics. Maybe it's because I'm Greek and I can't stop imagining carrying the torch someday, or maybe it's because secretly I want to be the one competing. Truth be told, it's probably both.

When I watch, I marvel at the strength of the competitors, at their determination. Even when I read about Olympic games gone by and famous athletes who beat the odds or made some amazing comeback to win a medal, I swell with pride.

One of my favorite Olympic stories involves a runner from Tanzania—John Stephen Akhwari—who competed in the 1968 Olympics in Mexico City. When he took part in the men's marathon, he started out as one of seventy-four participants set to run the 26.2-mile race. Together, the runners took off at 3:00 p.m., the hottest part of the day. A few hours later, everyone had either crossed the finish line or dropped out of the race. Everyone except John.

Early in the race, his calf muscle started cramping. Mexico City stands at an elevation of 7,350 feet. Tanzania stands at an elevation of 660 feet. John had not trained at altitude, and it affected his body. Almost to the halfway point, as he struggled to run with the cramping, there was some jockeying for position between runners. John was hit, and he fell hard onto the pavement, dislocating and wounding his knee and injuring his shoulder. After his wounds were bandaged on the sidelines, he stepped back into the race and kept running.

For almost an hour, John hobbled. And fell again. He got up and hobbled some more. At times he even dragged himself, only to rise up and stumble through. Officials begged him to stop. To drop out of the race. But he would not. When he finally shuffled into the stadium, most of the spectators had left. It had been almost a half hour since the last runner had crossed the finish line. But to the applause and cheers of the remaining fans, he limped over the finish line into the arms of medics.

When John was asked why he didn't drop out of the race, his answer said it all:

"My country did not send me to Mexico City to start the race; they sent me five thousand miles to finish the race."[2]

Can you imagine? I tear up just thinking about it! John's story went down in Olympic history and was dubbed "The Greatest Last Place Finish Ever." What a great description. I wonder—if he'd finished first and captured the gold medal, would he have ever realized what he was actually capable of doing? We'll never know, of course; but what has never left me about John's story is that in the face of such physical pain, such emotional pressure, such incredible adversity, something inside him kept him moving forward. Fueling his passion. Providing him strength against impossible odds. Helping him press on and push through when everything was working against him. Pushing him to finish the race he'd started. And while I have no way of knowing what all he drew on in those moments, I do recognize the strength he had.

From a spiritual standpoint, I want to be like John. Though I don't plan on running a marathon like he did, I am running a spiritual race here on earth. And as I run, I want to be full of vision, passion, determination, and courage.[3] I want to fulfill all the plans and purposes God has for my life. I want to stay on mission until I cross the finish line. No matter what gets thrown my way, or what tries to hold me back, I want to be like the apostle Paul when, at the end of his life, he wrote to his protégé Timothy and said, "I have fought the good fight, I have finished the race, I have kept the faith."[4] In order to do that, no doubt, I'm going to need something greater than me. Something internal *and* eternal. Something I can get only from God. The writer of Hebrews had a name for this something. He called it *endurance.*

"You have need of endurance, so that when you have done the will of God you may receive what is promised."[5]

Endurance. It's what you and I both need to keep moving forward in this life. Against all odds. Against all opposition. Against all setbacks, disappointments, and disillusionments. When nothing turns out like we expect. When, despite all the pain, we need to get back up and keep running our race. It's what we'll need to finish all that we start.

Endurance is formally defined as "the ability or strength to continue . . . despite fatigue, stress, or other adverse conditions."[6] It's the capacity to bear up under difficult circumstances. The power to withstand pain or hardships. It's a hopeful fortitude that perseveres to the end. In the original Greek language of the New Testament, it is *hupomone,* a compound word that translates "to remain under."[7] It is a quality built by remaining under pressure—something we naturally prefer to avoid.

I have spent a lifetime building endurance—mentally, emotionally, spiritually, and physically; and I have found they are all quite connected. When the global pandemic of 2020 began and quarantines went into effect, overnight, I was no longer able to travel and speak at live events, though I did record numerous messages for churches around the world. Because I was unexpectedly at home for months on end, my friend Dawn, who has walked, run, and hiked more trails than I ever will, invited me to start hiking the trails and mountains scattered throughout Southern California. *Why not?* I thought. *Since moving to the States, I've never had the time to explore the great outdoors. Now's my chance.* Little did I know how God was going to use such a decision.

Taking hold of Dawn's suggestion, I began prepping in every way I knew how. In every area I could, I began building stamina, strength, and courage to go a greater distance. To do what I had never done before. Deep inside, I knew that God wanted to increase my capacity, especially spiritually. As He'd used many other activities in my life, such as walking, running, weightlifting, and even boxing, this time He was going to use hiking. How, I had no idea, but I was up for it.

To be honest, as we ventured out on each of the hikes, weekend after weekend, I found myself thinking very little about God and spiritual principles. I was mostly trying to survive! Often we would trek for six to eight hours, climbing in elevation by as much as 4,500 feet in the span of a few short hours. Once we reached a summit, we would have to begin the equally dangerous trek downhill, which requires just as much skill, steadiness, and endurance as the ascent.

In the days following a hike, as I would rest and recover and go for long walks along the beach, I would begin to see volumes of spiritual truth. And out of that truth came this devotional—inspiration to help you build the endurance you need to run your race, fulfill all the purposes and plans God has for you, and stay on mission—even in the face of adversity. Especially in the face of adversity.

Together, we'll explore the many ways we endure, what hinders us from enduring, and how to make lasting change in our lives so we can endure. In short, I'll share with you all I learned putting one foot in front of the other while walking, running, and climbing the great outdoors of Southern California and beyond.

Love you so much,

Christine Caine

PART 1

FAITH, TRUST, AND STRENGTH

When you go to the mountains, you see them and you admire them. In a sense, they give you a challenge, and you try to express that challenge by climbing them.

EDMUND HILLARY

1 MARVELOUS FAITH

When [Jesus] was not far from the house, the centurion sent friends, saying to him, "Lord, do not trouble yourself, for I am not worthy to have you come under my roof. . . . But say the word, and let my servant be healed. . . ." When Jesus heard these things, he marveled at him, and turning to the crowd that followed him, said, "I tell you, not even in Israel have I found such faith."

LUKE 7:6–9 ESV

When Jesus encountered this centurion, He marveled at his faith. "Marveled" in the Greek is *thaumazo*, and it means "to be astonished, to be amazed." What on this earth could ever cause Jesus to be astonished or amazed? After all, He is the God of this universe. He existed always. He hung the stars and the moon. He's literally seen it all and *knows everything*. But for some reason, He marveled at the faith of a man who believed his servant could be healed. "Not even in Israel have I found such faith," Jesus said.

I want to have faith like the centurion—the kind that causes Jesus to marvel and say, "I haven't seen this kind of faith." I want to have such faith that I always believe God can do what He said He will do, no matter how impossible it may seem, naturally speaking. I want to have faith that there is no heart God cannot mend, no past He cannot redeem, no sickness He cannot heal, no relationship He cannot restore, no person

He cannot save, no sin He cannot forgive, no need He cannot meet, no prayer so big that He cannot answer it.

And yet to have that kind of faith is risky because it means trusting God and His Word. It means believing that God is good, that God does good, and that God is working all things together for my good, even when things don't look good. It means trusting that Jesus is who He says He is and that He will do what He said He would do, even when it takes much longer than I like or happens in a way I never imagined. It means pursuing Jesus when the world around me is constantly reminding me that my faith doesn't make sense. That it's foolish to believe in Jesus.

Trusting Jesus hasn't come easy for me. Still, I'm willing to risk it. What about you? Are you willing to risk believing more deeply than you ever have? No matter what hasn't gone according to plan in your life, the truth still stands: God created you on purpose for a purpose. He positioned you in time and gave you gifts and talents for the purpose of serving your generation. For having faith that endures despite setbacks and challenges. A faith that causes Him to marvel.

Heavenly Father, I commit this day to risk growing deeper in my faith than ever before. I want to fulfill all that You've called me to do, full of marvelous faith. In Jesus' name, amen.

2 ENDURING FAITH

We live by faith, not by sight.
2 CORINTHIANS 5:7 NIV

God has called us to live by faith and not by sight, though I feel sure we'd both agree there are times when that is easier said than done. There will always be situations we can't explain, when we will have to trust God with all our hearts and resist the temptation to exhaust ourselves trying to understand what we cannot. Tossing and turning in our sleep, ruminating on conversations and events and all the things we think we could have done differently will never help. I know because I've tried it, again and again, and it does no good—ever.

What does help is going to God in prayer and asking Him all the questions lingering in our hearts and minds, especially when we've gone through something that seems to test our faith. It's as though asking all the questions helps us wrestle with our faith so we can keep living by faith—even when we don't get perfectly clear answers.

I know in my own life I have a ton of unanswered questions from times when I've been hurt. When I've been betrayed. When I've been disappointed or disillusioned. When I've failed and things didn't go as I had expected or planned. When people I loved have died way too soon. When storms have come. When sickness has come. Still, God wants me to ask my questions—and He wants you to ask yours.

When we go to Him, we have to trust in His character, which means that despite what someone has done to us or what pain some circumstance has caused us, we trust in who God is: He is good, holy, faithful, kind, caring, loving, merciful, just, and in control.

Even in the times when we do receive answers, if we are to keep living by faith, our trust is to be in Him—not in the answers or in our understanding. Answers help, but they are not our source of enduring faith. He is.

Is there a lingering question on your mind today? Go ahead and ask Him. Even if it's something you've asked Him about a thousand times before. When you do, be willing to trust Him more than ever. Trust in His character. Trust in who He is. Be willing to live by faith and not by sight, today and forevermore.

Heavenly Father, I trust You and who You are. I put my trust in You, whether I ever understand everything that happens in my life or not. I live by faith and not by sight. In Jesus' name, amen.

3 LIVE BY FAITH

I have been crucified with Christ, and I no longer live, but Christ lives in me. The life I now live in the body, I live by faith in the Son of God, who loved me and gave himself for me.

GALATIANS 2:20

W e are living in a day and age where we as Christians are often considered foolish if we live by faith. Sometimes, in our schools, workplaces, and communities, we are surrounded by people who believe different things, and we can be considered foolish to believe in Jesus and all that He can do in us and through us. Having grown up in Australia, a nation where less than 2 percent of the people even go to church, I'm used to it. I determined long ago that nothing will stop me from living by faith.

For example, when people ask me if I really believe the Bible, my answer is a quick yes. When they ask if I really believe Jesus' birth was the result of a virgin birth, it's a quick yes. When they ask me if I really believe Jesus died, was buried, and rose from the dead, it's a quick yes. You can ask me about anything in the Bible. Moses and the Red Sea. Jonah and the fish. Daniel and the lions' den. Pick a story—I believe them all!

Why? Because Christ lives in me and I live by faith. I may not understand it all, but I believe it all. I can't help but believe the world needs us to be people who believe God, who believe in God, who are willing to act on all that we say we believe and on all we profess to be truth from the Scripture. It's part of how we build endurance.

More than ever, I'm prepared to look foolish in these days, to be that person who is full of the joy of the Lord. Who is full of the love of God. Who is full of the courage, strength, and hope of the Lord. Who dares to believe our best days are ahead of us, and not behind us, solely because God is great. Because He is who He says He is. Because He will do what He says He will do.

Won't you join me? Together, let's renew our personal commitment to Jesus today. Let's remember that we have been crucified with Christ, and it is no longer we who live, but Christ who lives in us. Let's live by faith in the Son of God, who loved us and gave Himself for us.

Father, I am thankful that Christ lives in me. I have faith in You, and I renew my commitment to live by faith. In Jesus' name, amen.

4 EQUIPPED WITH FAITH

By the grace given to me, I tell everyone among you not to think of himself more highly than he should think. Instead, think sensibly, as God has distributed a measure of faith to each one.

ROMANS 12:3

One of the most important parts of hiking doesn't take place anywhere along the trail. It doesn't take place at the trailhead. It doesn't even take place on the way there. It takes place in the days and weeks ahead. So many times, when I was preparing to climb peaks in Southern California with my friend Dawn, she would send me texts telling me about where we would be going, what the climb in elevation would be, and how many miles we would walk. She would recommend supplements I could begin taking a few days ahead to deal with the altitude and what foods to pack so I stayed energized. She would tell me what to expect from the weather, and then remind me what kind of clothing to wear, what weight of jacket to bring, and what gear I would need.

I came to understand and appreciate that the right equipment is crucial to staying safe and being able to endure all day long—and to succeed at any hike, whether it's up a mountain, through a wilderness, or across a flat plain. I'll never forget when my husband, Nick, ordered me a new hydration vest and set of trekking poles for our Yosemite trip. I laughed at myself for how excited I got. Who knew equipment would be the key to my heart?

More than once, I've thought about this, and the spiritual implications haven't escaped me. God always ensures we have the right equipment for the life He's called us to live.

God has called us to live by faith, walk by faith, and stay in faith—and He's equipped each one of us with a measure of faith. That means He's given us all the faith we need to do what He's called us to do—and He's called us all to do something. He has plans and purposes for each of our lives. He has good works for us to do.

Do you know what God has called you to do? Does it feel like a mountain that's unscalable? They all look like that when you're at the bottom or somewhere in the middle. But I know from experience, if you will just reach in your pack and pull out what you've been given, if you'll risk activating the faith God's given you, you will accomplish all that He's called you to do.

Father, thank You for the measure of faith You have given me. I will risk trusting You and stepping out in faith to do all that You've called me to do. In Jesus' name, amen.

5 FAITH CALLS THINGS INTO EXISTENCE

As it is written: I have made you [Abraham] the father of many nations—in the presence of the God in whom he believed, the one who gives life to the dead and calls things into existence that do not exist.

ROMANS 4:17

W hen my mother passed away a number of years ago, it felt like a season when dominoes began falling, because her death not only brought on the grief you would expect; it also triggered grief for a woman I'd never met—my biological mother. I remember thinking, *Really, God? We have to go there? I'm in my fifties. Is this really necessary?*

Of course it was—because God always wants to go for another layer of healing in our lives. While I was grappling with all these emotions, about eight weeks later, a sister-in-law on my side of our family passed away too. Then, over the next year, we lost another sister-in-law on Nick's side, and one of his sisters.

In the midst of these losses, I was deeply hurt by a friend, and a project I had poured my heart and soul into didn't turn out the way I expected. It was a time when I needed my faith in Jesus most of all.

When we go through difficult times, our tendency can be to bury or deny or ignore our pain and go on, and then sometimes label that faith. But that isn't faith.

Faith isn't calling things that are as though they are not.

Faith is calling those things that are not as though they are.

That's what Abraham did when God promised him He'd make him the father of many nations. Though he was childless, and he and Sarah were past their childbearing years, he did not waver in unbelief. He didn't deny the reality of his circumstances. He was just fully convinced that what God had promised, God was able to do. And He did. He gave them a son in their old age.

When I was hurting, to say that I wasn't hurting would not have been faith. That would have been denial, and that would have gotten me nowhere good. It would have become like a festering wound and eventually seeped everywhere. Into my words. Into my actions. Perhaps as toxicity or negativity or hopelessness or despair.

But to invite Jesus in to heal me, to pray and ask for His help, to declare His truth over the facts—that was faith. That was calling those things that are not as though they are.

I don't know what losses you have endured or what challenges you might be facing today, but the way forward is to put your faith to work. To speak God's Word over your life and circumstances. To call things into existence that do not exist . . . yet.

Heavenly Father, I call things into my life that do not exist right now. I put my faith to work, trusting in You and what You will do for me. In Jesus' name, amen.

6 FAITH THAT WILL GET YOU THROUGH

If the God we serve exists, then he can rescue us from the furnace of blazing fire, and he can rescue us from the power of you, the king. But even if he does not rescue us, we want you as king to know that we will not serve your gods or worship the gold statue you set up.

DANIEL 3:17–18

Did you catch what today's scripture says? The king had thrown Daniel's three friends into the fire, and still they said that even if God did not rescue them, they wouldn't bow to the king's false gods. Their faith was unwavering. It was *even if* faith!

Even if faith is the kind of faith God wants us to have, because it's the kind of faith that will keep us grounded when we are in the midst of a crisis, when we do not understand what is going on, when our circumstances are painful, confusing, demoralizing, disheartening, or disappointing.

Even if faith is *now* faith! It's faith for the present moment and for whatever fiery trial we're going through, because, let's face it—we're always entering a fire, in the middle of a fire, or coming out of one. What are you facing today? Maybe you're going through a divorce. Maybe you've learned you can't graduate on time. Maybe you have been given a grim diagnosis. Maybe you've lost a dear friendship. Maybe you have lost your job. Lost your savings. Lost your business. Maybe you've lost someone you loved deeply. And the pain you are feeling is something you've never known and something you never want to feel again. The only kind of faith that will get you through is *even if* faith.

Sitting around looking for Jesus to come rescue us isn't going to equip us to walk through the fires, but *even if* faith will, because it's faith that endures.

Even if faith looks at life this way:

"*Even if* I can't finish school right now, yet I will trust God!"
"*Even if* the doctor calls and there's something seriously wrong, yet
    I will trust God!"
"*Even if* I lose my job, yet I will trust God!"
"*Even if* . . . yet I will trust God!"

That's the level of trust and kind of faith I want to have in God! Don't you? That's what will keep us moving forward full of strength. Yes, I understand that in the fiery furnace many times we will feel the heat of the flames. We will get scorched. We will not escape any of the pain, but we will have Jesus to get us through anything that comes our way.

Father, I declare today that I have even *if faith for what's before me. Whatever happens, yet I will trust You! In Jesus' name, amen.*

7 THE GAP OF FAITH

Faith is the reality of what is hoped for, the proof of what is not seen.
HEBREWS 11:1

Every time I plan a big hike, I watch videos of experienced hikers climbing the actual trail. I follow along as they point out challenging sections and give tips on how to navigate them. I take note when they mention dangerous drop-offs or unending switchbacks. And I always appreciate hearing the joy and excitement in their voices when they highlight the views they want to be sure no one misses.

It's how I prepare my mind and ramp up my enthusiasm for what I know won't be an easy trek but will be well worth it. It's how I build my confidence that I can do it, even though I know I will still be greatly challenged the whole way through. And when I'm actually on the trail, putting one foot in front of the other, I remember what I saw and heard in the video—and it keeps me going.

It's so similar to what I do to live and walk by faith. I encourage my faith in every way I can. I worship. I pray. I fellowship with other Christ followers. I go to God's Word, read it, meditate on it, memorize it . . . and when the pressure is on, the Holy Spirit reminds me of what I've read. I listen to preached messages and read books. Doing all these things regularly—though not necessarily in any particular order—keeps me going.

We have to strengthen our faith daily so when we're in that span of time between where we are and where we want to be, when we're in the gap between what is and what will be, between what is seen and what is unseen, we can keep going. We can endure.

Are you in that gap of faith right now? Maybe you're waiting on a promotion or a new job opportunity. Maybe you're waiting on a relationship to mend or a child to come home. Maybe you're waiting on your body to heal or your mind to recover. Whatever you're waiting on, keep living by faith. Keep walking by faith. Keep making decisions by faith. Because faith is the reality of what you hope for, the proof of what is not seen . . . but will be soon.

Father, thank You for the gift of faith. Thank You for helping me en-courage my faith so I can keep walking and living by faith. In Jesus' name, amen.

8 JUST KEEP WALKING

"Lord, if it's you," Peter answered him, *"command me to come to you on the water." He said, "Come." And climbing out of the boat, Peter started walking on the water and came toward Jesus.*

MATTHEW 14:28–29

When was the last time Jesus invited you to step out of the boat and start walking on water? You know what I mean. When has He asked you to take a step of faith and you knew it wouldn't be just one step; it would be two, then three, then four . . . and you knew that to keep going would require even more faith?

I know how scary it can feel to take that first step, and all the subsequent steps, but I've been taking steps almost all my adult life, ever since I gave my heart fully to Jesus. I feel as if every day I have to trust Jesus to show up in every realm of my life, because I'm so far out in the water there's no turning back. There's no one else to depend on. There's no one else big enough, powerful enough, gracious enough, but Jesus.

It's an exhilarating ride that Jesus offers us, to walk by faith, to trust Him to get so far out that there's no one and nothing else to trust. At this stage of my life, I've learned that when He asks me to do something, it will require faith once more, and most likely it will be because it's an impossible assignment. I often remind our team around the world that I'm not asking them to do difficult things. I'm asking them to do impossible things and to walk in the faith God's given them. To step out of every boat they find themselves in and start walking on water. Because if they will do that, Jesus will be there. He does the miraculous for us. Yes, we will feel the fear of the first step—and the next. We may feel unbalanced. Our minds may swirl with all the what-if scenarios. We might even come unhinged a time or two, but one step back doesn't mean we can't take two steps forward. And then some more. After all, we're people of faith who live by faith and walk by faith, aren't we?

Whatever it is that Jesus has put in your heart to do, whatever you are in the midst of doing for His kingdom and for His glory, keep doing it by faith. Keep stepping out of the boat and walking on water. Dare to keep walking, to get so far out in the water you can't see the boat, the shore, or any of the lifesavers you've once depended on. If you will, Jesus will be there!

Jesus, I choose today to step out of the boat once more. To walk toward You on the water once more. And most of all, to keep walking in ways I never have before. In Jesus' name, amen.

9 THE HAND OF GOD

*"If it pleases the king, and if your servant has found favor with you, send me
to Judah and to the city where my ancestors are buried, so that I may rebuild
it. . . . If it pleases the king, let me have letters written to the governors
of the region . . . And let me have a letter written to Asaph, keeper of the
king's forest, so that he will give me timber to rebuild the gates of the temple's
fortress, the city wall, and the home where I will live." The king granted my
requests, for the gracious hand of my God was on me.*
NEHEMIAH 2:5–8

God has given you an assignment; in fact, He's given every one of
us an assignment. And to successfully fulfill what He's called us
to do, we need His favor. No doubt, often what God gives us to do is
impossible. It was for Nehemiah. He wanted to rebuild the wall around
Jerusalem, and he certainly couldn't do it alone. He needed timber,
people to help, tools, and time. When he asked for all those things, the
king granted them—because of God's favor, because of God's hand on
Nehemiah.

In most everything I have done, I have asked God for His favor
because I know I can't succeed and endure here on earth without it. In
every assignment, I have dared to believe God would open doors for me
that were previously shut tight—and close ones I didn't need to walk
through. I've prayed for favor with people I meet and work with that

together we would get more done for the kingdom. I'm not saying God has always done it the way I imagined or given me what I wanted the way I wanted it, but I have found that the more I ask for His favor, the more I see results—and each time He gives me the grace to accept how those results come.

Have you ever prayed for God's favor? Do you remember what it felt like when whatever you were sweating, God moved? Even when He shut a door? That was His favor at work in your life. God is so gracious that He gives His favor freely to us all. I can't tell you how much I have built my life and ministry around that last phrase, "for the gracious hand of my God was on me."

Do you feel God's hand on your life? If you aren't sure what that feels like, look for it today. Watch for all the ways He works things out on your behalf. Watch for the ways people grant you opportunities. Watch for how God reroutes you so you succeed at your job, at your calling, and in your purpose. That's the hand of God. It's His favor on your life.

Father, thank You for Your favor on my life. Help me be aware of it so I can give You all the glory for all You do. In Jesus' name, amen.

10 YOU CAN HAVE SUCCESS

"This book of instruction must not depart from your mouth; you are to meditate on it day and night so that you may carefully observe everything written in it. For then you will prosper and succeed in whatever you do."
JOSHUA 1:8

G od created us for success. In fact, other translations of today's verse say God created us to have good success.[8] Good success is not success as the world might define it, as having the best or the biggest, or being first or the fastest. Based on this verse, good success is becoming what God wants us to become. It's doing what God created us to do while we live here on earth.

In my life, I pray for my girls that they will have success at school. I pray for my husband that he would have success in leading our teams and doing all that God has called him to do. I pray for success for our staff. I don't believe God wants any of them to have a mediocre life. I believe that God wants them to have victorious, overcoming, passionate, purpose-driven, faith-filled lives that are full of good success! I believe that He wants this for every single one of us.

When it comes to the work God has called me to do, I pray for great opportunities. I want to reach as many people as I can in my lifetime with the good news of the gospel of Jesus Christ.

I pray for good success in things that probably matter to no one but me, because I know that God really does care about things that matter to us that might not seem important to anyone else. Before I go out to tackle another mountain, I pray to God that I will have success to get all the way to the summit and all the way back down . . . alive. With no injuries. Without passing out. Not having been bitten by a snake or chased by a mountain lion or terrified by a bear.

If you've never prayed for God to give you good success—or maybe you haven't in a while—pray this way today. I think it is so important to our enduring in faith that we continue to elevate our expectations, that we stretch our faith, so we can be more effective for the kingdom. Whatever we've done for God already, I believe we can do more, even if we've hit those years when people think we should wind down. As long as we're still alive, there's still purpose for us to fulfill. We can't all do everything, but we can all do something. And in that something, we can have good success!

Father, thank You for giving me success in everything You've called me to do. Help me to be mindful of Your plans and purposes for my life, for every day of my life. In Jesus' name, amen.

11 GO AGAIN

He said to his servant, "Go up and look toward the sea." So he went up,
looked, and said, "There's nothing." Seven times Elijah said, "Go back."
On the seventh time, he reported, "There's a cloud as small as a man's hand
coming up from the sea."
1 KINGS 18:43–44

S even times! That's how many times Elijah sent his servant to go
and see if there was any rain coming. There was a severe drought
and famine throughout the land of Samaria, and God had promised rain,
but time after time, when Elijah sent his servant to go up and look toward
the sea, there was nothing in sight.

Have you ever been there? When God's given you a promise? When
He's dropped something into your heart from His Word? When you've
prayed and prayed for it? When you've waited and waited for it? When
you've strained to see over the horizon, hoping to get a glimpse of it, but
every time you go and look, you see nothing?

Maybe you're watching for your son or daughter to come back to
Jesus. Maybe you're working hard for the resources to buy a house or get
your children through college. Maybe you're waiting for the right time
to start a new venture you've dreamed about for years.

I know what waiting feels like, and I have found that there's nothing
that will challenge your faith like waiting and seeing nothing. Especially

if it's about a promise that goes unfulfilled for weeks and months and even years. So much of what I have been able to see happen began as a seed God dropped into my heart decades ago, as far back as when I was ministering to youth in the country towns of Australia. Many times, there was no evidence that anything would ever come to pass. Still, I just knew the things He had put in my heart, so I kept praying His promises and believing Him for the rain. I kept watching for it. Just as Elijah kept sending his servant to do.

On the seventh time, the servant finally saw something. He saw a cloud as small as a man's hand coming up from the sea. It was a glimmer of hope. A tiny cloud. It wasn't the rain that had been promised, not yet, but it was a sign that a downpour could come—and soon it did.

Whatever God has dropped into your heart to do, whatever the promise is that you're praying will happen, go again to the sea's horizon to look for rain. And again. And again. Keep enduring and going as many times as it takes until you see a glimpse of the promise. Until you begin to see the rain.

Father, thank You for the promise You have given me. I will keep going in faith, looking over the horizon, watching for a glimpse of it for as long as it takes. I have enduring faith. In Jesus' name, amen.

12 FAITH FILLS THE SPACE

Do everything without grumbling and arguing, so that you may be blameless and pure, children of God who are faultless in a crooked and perverted generation, among whom you shine like stars in the world, by holding firm to the word of life.

PHILIPPIANS 2:14–16

My daughters are both teenagers, and although I'm the kind of mother who likes to have a place for everything and everything in its place, neither of them seems to have inherited my inclination for that kind of organization. I see glimpses of it here and there, and I risk getting my hopes up that change has come, but most of the time all I see is laundry scattered across their bedroom floors.

Though I've placed laundry baskets in their rooms to encourage them to discover the wonder of order, for some reason they still prefer their dirty clothes outside the basket.

For the longest time, when I would look in their rooms, I would grumble and complain at all I saw wrong—namely, the clothes on the floor—but I was missing too much. I wasn't seeing their love for all their friends and family in the pictures they'd placed on the walls. I wasn't seeing their diligence and hard work in all the schoolwork spread out on the desks. I wasn't seeing their creativity in the outfits stretched across their beds.

One day, after hearing me vent again, Nick—who often sounds a lot like the Holy Spirit—kindly made a suggestion that got my attention: "Chris, what if you start thanking God that you've got kids, and that they've got clothes for you to pick up, rather than stressing over it so much?"

It was so simple. And he was so right. Sure, they needed to exercise discipline and clean up their rooms, but in that season of time, I was making too big a deal of it. And it was draining us all.

As I quit grumbling and complaining, I began to do the opposite. I spoke words of life and faith—enduring in faith even when I saw the empty laundry baskets and the clothes all over the floor—and the atmosphere in our home changed, as did the condition of my heart. I felt a discernible shift in my whole attitude. I noticed that the time I had been taking to complain was soon replaced with an awe and wonder at the wonderful young women my girls had become. Faith filled the space where negativity once was. And I couldn't miss everything else positive I saw in their rooms.

Do you want the atmosphere where you live or work or volunteer to change? Do what I did. Start speaking words of life and faith—and watch faith fill the space.

Father, I commit to speaking words of life and faith today. I will call out the goodness that's around me and look forward to faith filling the space. In Jesus' name, amen.

13 A SEED OF FAITH

"Because of your little faith," he told them. "For truly I tell you, if you have faith the size of a mustard seed, you will tell this mountain, 'Move from here to there,' and it will move. Nothing will be impossible for you."

MATTHEW 17:20

Faith is the currency of heaven. It's what moves God. And when God is moved, He moves mountains. He's looking for people who are willing to have faith, and from what He said, faith the size of a tiny mustard seed will work. Even when we're facing the impossible.

I find this such good news because so much in my life started with something small. I remember when I first started learning about the Bible, before I could quote any of the passages I know today, I started with memorizing one verse. Just one.

When I started speaking, I began with six young girls in a discipleship group. They were part of the larger youth group at our church, but they were the first I got to pour my life into. I spoke to them with the same passion I speak with today.

When I wrote my first book, it was by writing one word at a time. And a few words grew into a sentence, and a few sentences grew into a paragraph, and those paragraphs grew into pages, which became chapters. To this day, when I start a new book, it's the very same way, with lots of writing and rewriting and ruthless editing. I'd love to tell you that

I've progressed to where I just close my eyes, pray, and it all just comes to me, but it's never happened that way.

My messages are the same. They start small. They start with prayer and study, with time spent in the Word. They start with seeking God, and then, as the Holy Spirit gives me ideas, I make notes.

Even when we started the work of A21, the anti–human trafficking organization Nick and I founded, we began with rescuing one person from human trafficking. Not the hundreds that we have rescued since. Not the thousands we have helped avoid it. Not the millions we have educated about it. At the beginning, we helped just one.

In every area of our lives, big things always start small, and as we keep enduring in faith, they grow. What has God put in your heart to do? Has He given you a business idea? An educational goal? A fitness goal? Maybe He's given you a book to write, an invention to pursue, or a product to manufacture. I've got good news for you! Start where you are with what you have. Start with the seed of faith God has given you. From what He's said, I know it's the perfect size.

Father, thank You for the faith You've given me and that it is more than enough to do all You've called me to do. Show me how to start where I am with what I have. I'm ready! In Jesus' name, amen.

14 ENDURANCE
SUSTAINS OUR FAITH

You need endurance, so that after you have done God's will, you may receive what was promised.
HEBREWS 10:36

I love to land in a new city, lace up my running shoes, and hit the pavement, though many times it has led to unexpected adventures. You would think that I'd learn, but on more than one occasion I've gotten lost and had to run much farther than I ever thought I could to find my way back to where I started. It's been in those moments, when I've exhausted myself to the point that I didn't think I could take another step, that I've imagined myself a marathon runner who's hit a wall and has to power on through the miles. It's a grand illusion, I know, since I'm not *that* serious of a runner. Still, I have known what it's like to think I'm going to collapse. That I can't possibly go on. That I can't keep going. And yet, each time, I have found the strength.

I have found the same to be true as I have run my spiritual race in faith. So many times, I have hit a wall and thought, *I'm done. I can't go on. I can't go one more step.* And yet, somehow, someway, I did—though it was never in my own strength. Pushing through whatever was in front of me has produced a strength in my life that can't be produced any other way. It's produced *endurance,* something Scripture said we would have need of, something that keeps us going even when we don't think we can keep going.

It works the same in all our lives. When we push through over and over, we grow stronger spiritually and we build endurance, a critical component that sustains our faith. *Endurance* is "the ability to withstand hardship or adversity."[9] It's the capacity and power to bear up under difficult circumstances. It's a hopeful fortitude that perseveres to the end. It is a quality built by remaining under pressure, something our natural inclination wants to drift away from.

Don't we all want to escape when the pressure becomes too great? I know I do, but I did not build spiritual strength by doing the things that came easy to me, but by overcoming the things I did not think I could. It's how I grew in faith. I feel sure it's how you've grown in your faith too.

Hold on to that understanding today. Whatever is bearing down on you, keep enduring. Keep putting your trust in the One who is faithful to do as He's promised.

Heavenly Father, thank You for all the endurance that's been built into my life and for how it sustains my faith. I choose to keep enduring, trusting You that I will receive what You've promised. In Jesus' name, amen.

15 TRUST HIM MORE

"As heaven is higher than earth, so my ways are higher than your ways, and my thoughts than your thoughts."
ISAIAH 55:9

After more than thirty years of following Jesus, there is much I still don't understand, but God's ways are not my ways, and His thoughts are not my thoughts. In fact, Isaiah wrote that they are both higher than mine. So my starting point in wading through any confusion I might have is that God is God, and I am not. If I do not understand something God is doing, it does not suggest a problem with God. It just means I don't get it. At least, not at the moment.

I have consistently found that we rarely have the whole picture all at once. It's as if we're holding a piece of a jigsaw puzzle and God is holding the other 999 pieces that we don't even know exist yet. We can't see all that He is doing. But just because we can't see all these things doesn't mean we shouldn't have faith in God and trust Him and believe that He is working.

Still, I know it's not always easy. I've always been the kind of person who is more likely to take matters into my own hands than to trust God. It shows up in my life when I focus too much on people acting in predictable ways, or liking things done a certain way and everything being in its place. Without meaning to, I can get obsessed with schedules and plans. I guess you could say, without Jesus, I can be a bit of a control freak; but to be honest, it's not entirely without reason. After years of doing the hard work of learning to trust God through every unknown—to embrace the pain of healing and recovery time and time again—I have come to understand that some of my control tendencies have their origin in coping mechanisms, ones I developed because of some of the trauma I experienced in my past.

Still, God invites me to trust Him, just as He invites us all, regardless of what we've been through. He wants us to grow from one place of faith to the next, building endurance along the way.

So how do you respond when you find yourself facing an opportunity to trust God more? Do you tend to start controlling when you'd really rather be trusting Him? At some point, we all have to surrender our attempts to control everything and everyone and learn how to place all our trust in Him. I'm so grateful God never gives up on us. That He never stops helping us live and walk by faith, no matter how many times we take matters into our own hands.

Heavenly Father, You are so merciful. Thank You for always being so patient with me as I learn to trust You more and try to control my world, and everyone in it, less. In Jesus' name, amen.

16 STAY CONFIDENT

Remember the earlier days when, after you had been enlightened, you endured a hard struggle with sufferings. Sometimes you were publicly exposed to taunts and afflictions . . . [You] accepted with joy the confiscation of your possessions, because you know that you yourselves have a better and enduring possession. So don't throw away your confidence, which has a great reward.
HEBREWS 10:32–35

There are few things I love more than running along the coast when the sun is setting. God's paintbrush strokes across the vast canvas of the unending sky are always stunning. It's as though it was all designed to help me forget that I'm actually gulping for air, sweating off toxins, and exhausting myself completely.

For more than three decades, I have laced up my running shoes and raced out the door. To detox. To cleanse. To absorb. To explore. To keep my feet on the ground, in every way. Physically. Mentally. Emotionally. Spiritually. It's something my soul and my body seem to need.

From running for so many years, I've built up a level of endurance that fuels my ability to keep going when I feel I've run out of strength—both mentally and physically. More than once, when I've set out on an unfamiliar trail, I've run far more steps than I planned and I've hit a wall—that place runners hit when they feel they can't keep going. But each time I push through and go the distance.

Endurance builds our confidence—our faith—in God, something the writer of Hebrews cautioned us not to lose. I have found that endurance and faith go together. We can't have one without the other. We can't build one without the other. When we feel we've hit a wall, and all we want to do is quit, we need to remember why it's important that we don't.

I like how the writer of Hebrews begins today's verses with the word *remember*. Sometimes, we just need to remember how far we've come to run the next leg of our race. There are times when I'm facing a challenge spiritually that I stop and remember all God has done in me, for me, and through me in the past, and it far outweighs what I might be facing in the present. It builds my confidence to keep going. To keep moving forward by faith.

What about you? Are you in a place where you need to endure but everything is screaming at you to quit? God wants you to keep going, full of faith and hope. Start remembering and keep walking by faith. Don't throw away your confidence!

Thank You, Father, for all the times You've helped me keep going, keep overcoming, with enduring faith. I am confident in You to do all that You have promised. In Jesus' name, amen.

17 TURN UP YOUR HEARING

Faith comes from what is heard, and what is heard comes through the message about Christ.

ROMANS 10:17

M ost of us are today the sum total of what we have heard and believed about ourselves. We enter the world a blank slate, and what we believe about ourselves and our destiny comes from what we hear.

If we have been encouraged, affirmed, and esteemed as children, and told that we are created by God for an awesome destiny, it's much easier to have the faith to believe it.

But if all we have heard is that we are useless, hopeless, not intelligent enough, the wrong color or ethnicity, or that we come from the wrong side of the tracks, we tend to believe those negative things that have been said to us, don't we?

Today's verse shows us that faith for success or failure comes by what is heard, and what is heard comes through the message about Christ. What are you hearing on a daily basis? People and their opinions? News stories? Office gossip? While we can't change what we've heard in the past or what we're hearing in the present, the understanding is that we have the power to choose what we will listen to in the midst of all the noise.

For someone like me who grew up hearing all the ways I fell short, this is such good news! I don't have to believe the negative things that were said about me or to me—and I don't have to believe everything I hear to this day.

When I gave my heart fully to God, decades ago, I began to listen to something completely new. I began listening to the truth found in God's Word—and I've never stopped. It continues to heal me, liberate me, encourage me, and give me faith for the present and for the future. It gives me faith to endure and live strong.

What are you listening to? The voices of the past? The lies you grew up believing? The negativity of friends? The voices on social media? The news you scroll through? Change what you're listening to. Fill your heart and mind and ears with the Word of God. You can read it. You can listen to it. You can memorize it, so you can say it to yourself. Faith comes from what you listen to, so listen to the message of Christ found in the Word.

Heavenly Father, thank You for giving me the ability to grow in my faith by listening to the voice of Your Word more than all the other voices. Thank You for Your Word. In Jesus' name, amen.

18 TO THE TOP

Consider it a great joy, my brothers and sisters, whenever you experience various trials, because you know that the testing of your faith produces endurance.

JAMES 1:2–3

Except for a rare few people in this world, life generally does not go as planned. It's full of curve balls, unexpected challenges, loss, disappointment, grief, and turmoil. My own life has been anything but trouble-free and pain-free, but looking back, I can definitely say that the decades I've spent with Jesus have certainly been better than my early years, when I lived without Him.

I would love to say I've discovered an easy path forward, but I haven't, and experience and Scripture have shown me it is not likely I will. We live in a fallen world, and trials are part of living here. Therefore, we will have troubles; we will make mistakes; we will experience disappointments; we will have loss; we will grow weary; we will hit spiritual walls; and we may even want to quit. Multiple times. But for all those times, Jesus has provided endurance, something James said comes when our faith is tested.

If only endurance were an app! Wouldn't it be great if we could just tap it open and request it like we do everything else we need? If we want a ride, there's an app. If we want to make reservations at a restaurant, there's an app. If we want groceries, a TV show, or a movie, there's an app. But for endurance, there is no app. I've checked!

Endurance is a strength that can be built only when we stay with something when all we really want to do is quit. It is a strength that is only built through resistance. Believe me: every time my trainer adds more weight to the bar, I groan. But my muscles will only grow stronger if I push against more resistance.

So it is with our spiritual life. One trial strengthens us for another. One testing of our faith prepares us for the next testing of our faith—to the point that there is a cumulative effect building endurance in us.

Take a moment and ask yourself how you look at trials in your life. Do you see them as a reason to stop taking risks and stepping out in faith? Do you see them as a reason to pull back instead of moving forward? It's much easier to let our feelings and desires take us wherever they are going, especially when we've been hurt. But Jesus wants us to move forward. He wants us to count it all joy, knowing that the testing of our faith produces endurance.

Father, You are so good. I consider it joy when I experience trials because I understand that the testing of my faith produces endurance—the very thing I need to keep living by faith. In Jesus' name, amen.

19 TIME TO BREAK THROUGH

Jericho was strongly fortified because of the Israelites—no one leaving or entering. The LORD said to Joshua, "Look, I have handed Jericho, its king, and its best soldiers over to you."

JOSHUA 6:1–2

When the children of Israel left the wilderness and crossed over into the promised land, the first thing they ran into was a wall surrounding the city of Jericho. They had spent forty years wandering in the wilderness, finally making it to their destination, and suddenly there was a wall. It was the most fortified wall ever constructed up to that time. It was actually two walls running parallel to one another. The outer wall was twenty feet tall and six feet thick. The inner wall was thirty feet tall and twenty feet thick.[10] From a human perspective, it was an unconquerable wall. Impenetrable. Impossible.

Can you imagine how they must have felt? They had experienced miracle after miracle since leaving Egypt, and just when they crossed over the Jordan River and things were finally going really well, they hit the mother of all walls. It was the last thing they expected to see.

Have you ever felt that way? Like everything was going really great and—bam!—you hit a wall you never saw coming? Maybe it wasn't made of brick and mortar, but it was still a wall because it was something that made you want to quit or, at the very least, slow down and pull back. It could have been spiritual, mental, or physical—and it felt as real as the walls around Jericho.

Maybe your wall has confused you . . . about God. About His character. About His nature. Maybe it has rocked your faith or caused you to doubt that you were in the will of God. Maybe it has left you feeling paralyzed from believing things could get better. It's so easy to feel this way when life doesn't go as we hope. God understands our pain and our disappointment, and He never leaves us.

Right after the children of Israel hit their wall, God said to Joshua, "Look, I have handed Jericho, its king, and its best soldiers over to you." What a promise! What perspective! Can you imagine what that did for their faith? God didn't lead them all the way to the promised land just to hit a wall and quit. He led them all that way to take Jericho and then to keep going.

God wants the same for you. Whatever wall you've hit, it's not time to pull back. It's time to break through. Go to His Word. Look for His perspective. Find His promises for your situation and hold on to them with enduring faith until you see all that He has for you.

Father, I'm so glad You know every wall before I hit it, and You are there! Thank You for going before me and helping me live and walk by faith through every circumstance. In Jesus' name, amen.

20 A BOWLFUL OF BROCCOLI

The Lord God is a sun and shield. The Lord grants favor and honor; he does not withhold the good from those who live with integrity.
PSALM 84:11

On more than one occasion, when my girls were younger, I've had to explain that no matter how much we want to, and no matter how much we love the taste of it, we cannot live on salted caramel ice cream. You can imagine their shock and disappointment. The groaning and sighing that would follow never escaped me, though I grew strong early on in my motherly resolve.

I would often go on to explain that we had to eat vegetables more and ice cream less. But in the fairness of full disclosure, I'll admit I was just as disappointed as they were. I would much rather eat salted caramel ice cream any day over a vegetable. Wouldn't you? Why is it so much easier to pick the things that make us feel better than to pick the things that are better for us?

Isn't this the same struggle we face spiritually? How many times have we gone to God and essentially said, "God, here is my prayer request, and I just want You to know that all I like is salted caramel ice cream. I don't like vegetables. Therefore, whatever You do, answer me, but don't answer me with any vegetables."

And, in so many words, God answers us like any good parent would: "I know what's best for you. Here's a bowlful of broccoli. You might not like the taste of it, but trust Me: it's going to make you function the best. Don't you realize that I'm good and I know what's good for you? I'm not hurting you with the broccoli. I'm strengthening you. I'm preparing you for the future I've already prepared for you."

God does not withhold *the good* from us. But when He gives us vegetables instead of ice cream, that's exactly what we think. We think He's withholding from us or holding out on us. Are you as guilty of this as I am?

What if we started today trusting Him and His processes even more? All He's doing is what's best for us. He's being faithful to us. He's protecting us. He's stretching our faith. He's building endurance inside us. He's being a good Father who's working all things for our good, even when we don't like the taste of it . . . or the way it feels.

If He's just given you a bowlful of broccoli, trust that He's strengthening you. He's preparing you for the future He's already prepared for you. He's showing you His faithfulness.

Heavenly Father, thank You for Your devotion to me. Thank You that You give me only what is best for me because You're preparing me for the future You have prepared for me. In Jesus' name, amen.

21 NEVER LOOK BACK

"Remember Lot's wife!"

LUKE 17:32

Did you know this is the second-shortest verse in the Bible? Memorize it now and you could win the next Bible quiz! In the middle of talking all about the coming of the kingdom, Jesus says to remember Lot's wife. Why remember her? Of all people? There are more than 170 women mentioned in the Bible, and she is the only one Jesus tells us to remember. Not Mary, His mother. Not any of His sisters. Not any of the women He ministered to and with. Not one of the women in the Old Testament. He just tells us to remember Lot's wife—a woman who appeared on the pages of Scripture only long enough to disappear. All we know about her is that she looked back at Sodom and Gomorrah—after an angel took her by the hand and told her and her family to run for their lives—and she turned into a pillar of salt.

Jesus said to remember *her*.

Maybe it's because she did the one thing she was told not to do. Can't you just see her, lagging behind Lot, lingering a little, longing for her home? Perhaps the real issue was that she was torn between where she was leaving and where she was going. Perhaps her heart was still in Sodom with her friends and family and all the memories there. God had supernaturally turned up and told her to move on, and yet she still hovered in that place of indecision. Whatever it was, wanting what she had more than what God had ahead for her cost her life.

What has God asked you to do? What's He shown you for your future? Are you looking ahead or looking back? Are you stuck somewhere in the middle between what you had and what God has ahead for you? Are you stuck in a place mentally? Emotionally? Spiritually? Physically? Wherever you are on the journey, today is a good day to keep looking straight ahead and keep moving forward.

God has works for us to do. He wants us to live fruitful lives. When God is getting ready to move us forward, let us not ever be found losing such an opportunity. Let's keep enduring in faith. Let's have the courage to go where we have never gone before and to do what we have never done before. Let's have the courage to trust the hand of God holding us and guiding us into our future. Let's trust the love of God that is never ending and unfailing. There's no doubt that it is hard to leave what we're still connected to, but let's remember Lot's wife, just as Jesus said. Let's keep moving and never look back.

Heavenly Father, help me keep my eyes on You. Please help me re-member Lot's wife and not look back. I want to move forward into all the plans You have for my life. In Jesus' name, amen.

22 SOMETHING LESS OR SOMETHING MORE

Since we also have such a large cloud of witnesses surrounding us, let us lay aside every hindrance and the sin that so easily ensnares us. Let us run with endurance the race that lies before us.

HEBREWS 12:1

When I read the first line of today's verse, I imagine all the saints who have gone before us, who are leaning over the balcony of heaven, cheering us on. I also think of our brothers and sisters in Christ who are still on this earth and one step ahead of us. The ones who have been through what we might be going through, and they're telling us how they made it so we can make it too. Then, I notice the writer's advice in the next phrase: *Lay aside every hindrance and the sin that so easily ensnares us.*

Have you ever wondered how these thoughts fit together? I have, and I discovered that in the fifth century, Olympic athletes ran naked. They would enter the stadium wearing robes and drop them at the start of the race, because the lack of weight and resistance enabled them to run more efficiently. The writer of Hebrews used this athletic imagery to show us something: to run our spiritual race on this earth with endurance, we are going to have to drop anything that hinders us from running our race and fulfilling our purpose.

Could it be that there are relationships, habits, attractions, distractions, thoughts, even heart attitudes holding us back? Could it be there are sins interfering with our purpose? Our destiny? Could it be that we need to make some changes to align ourselves more closely to God's character? Maybe we're harboring anger, unforgiveness, or bitterness that we need to let go. Maybe there's jealousy or gossip we need to stop. Maybe there's insecurity or shame we need to invite Him in to heal. Overcoming things like this is often a process, but it's important to start it.

When God challenges me to lay something down—including good things, like activities I enjoy or foods I love—it's a step of faith, because faith is trusting that what God has for me is better than what I am laying down. The same is true for us all, because He loves each and every one of us and wants the best for us.

What has God been asking you to lay down? Have you felt a nudge to let something go? To do something less and something else more? Do you trust that God's purpose is better than your plan? Take a step of faith and risk giving in to His leading today. Then you can keep running with endurance the race that lies before you.

Heavenly Father, I want Your plans and Your purposes for my life more than the hindrances and sins that ensnare me. Help me identify what holds me back so I can step forward in faith. In Jesus' name, amen.

23 WHERE ARE YOU LOOKING?

. . . keeping our eyes on Jesus, the pioneer and perfecter of our faith. For the joy that lay before him, he endured the cross, despising the shame, and sat down at the right hand of the throne of God.

HEBREWS 12:2

Over the course of a weekend, Nick and I completed a motorcycle training course. He knows my love for Vespa riding and all things Italian, and he was kind enough to indulge me.

On the first day of our course, the emphasis was on vision, on looking and seeing what's in front of you, what's around you, and what's coming up behind you. But the very first thing they taught us was the biggest lesson of the day: where you look is where you will go.

What a lesson for our spiritual lives. What are we looking at day in and day out? Is that where we want to go? We live in an age where there are a multitude of options. We can spend hours a day looking at our phones. Looking at our email, how many likes we get and how many people are sharing our posts. Looking at the news and live-streaming shows. If we don't intentionally put our phones down, we might not ever stop.

The writer of Hebrews might not have had a clue what was coming in our generation, but he wrote knowingly for us to keep our eyes on Jesus. How important it is, then, to train our eyes to look away from everything else and to focus on Jesus first and foremost. We live in an age when technology has the power to distract us more than ever. Don't get me wrong; I couldn't do all that I do without my phone. It's how I communicate most of the time with our global team. Jumping on Zoom for a meeting is how we stay connected. And when Nick and I travel, we text or FaceTime with our girls daily. But despite how much we rely on technology to do all that God has called us to do, we can't let it consume so much of us that we forget to look to Jesus most of all.

Let's remember that Jesus is the reason we started. Jesus is the reason we keep going. Jesus is the reason we get back up. Jesus is the reason we do not stop.

If where you are looking has diverted you away from all that God has created you to be, from all He has called you to do, realign your focus. Look to Jesus, the pioneer and perfector of our faith. The One who endured so that we could too.

Jesus, I look to You. I turn my eyes toward You. And I won't look away. You are the reason I started and the reason I will keep going, living by faith. In Your name I pray, amen.

24 BE A BELIEVING BELIEVER

He was not able to do a miracle there, except that he laid his hands on a few sick people and healed them. And he was amazed at their unbelief. He was going around the villages teaching.

MARK 6:5–6

There are two times the Bible says Jesus was amazed. Once was when He encountered the faith of an unbeliever—the centurion. (You can review this on Day 1.) And once was when He went back to His hometown and taught in the synagogue. On that day, rather than receive from His teachings, many who heard Jesus questioned how He could possibly be qualified to teach. After all, He was the local carpenter's son, and they took offense at Him.

What irony. Here were the people of God, the Israelites from Jesus' hometown, gathered to hear the Word of God, but because they had become so familiar with Jesus, they didn't believe that He was who He said He was, or that He could do what He said He could do. The result? "He was not able to do a miracle there, except that he laid his hands on a few sick people and healed them."

It may be surprising, but apparently, there is a kind of unbelief that thwarts the work of God in a place. From what we read in the surrounding text of today's verse, it's rooted in familiarity with Jesus, and it breeds a laziness in our faith.

I don't believe any of us wants our familiarity with Jesus to cause us to have the kind of cynical unbelief that thwarts the plans and purposes of God. I don't believe any of us wants to grow lazy in our faith. Why would we? None of us wants to be like the people in Jesus' hometown, the ones we could call unbelieving believers, because, in a sense, that's what they were. They believed enough to come hear Jesus but not enough to activate all that He wanted to do for them.

Let's be believing believers who have the kind of faith that activates marvelous works, miracles, signs, and wonders. Let's be believing believers who receive all that Jesus has to say and all He wants to do. Is there something specific you need from Him today? Dare to have the kind of faith that amazes Him, and watch what He will do!

Dear Jesus, I am a believing believer! I believe You are who You say You are, and You will do what You say You will do. Especially in my life today. In Jesus' name, amen.

25 FAITH TO FINISH

I am able to do all things through him who strengthens me.

PHILIPPIANS 4:13

The terrain was treacherous. Steep. Uneven. A bit rocky. I was hiking down Mount Baden Powell, one of the first mountains I ever climbed, and it was nothing like I had imagined. For some reason, though I'd watched videos to prepare and listened carefully to all my friend Dawn had warned me about, I still thought hiking down the mountain would be easier than hiking up the mountain. After all, I'd have gravity on my side, right? To my way of thinking, it would be faster. It only made sense. But like everything else in life, until we experience something for ourselves, our understanding often falls short.

Following Dawn's lead, studying her technique, I dug in my trekking poles before each step, taking the time to stabilize one foot before moving the other. Though I wanted to look up and out, I didn't dare; one misstep and I might go tumbling. It was such a laborious and painstaking process, one that required more patience than I like to exercise. I was surprised to realize our descent was requiring much of me, just as hiking to the summit had; but unlike the trek up, I was no longer charged with energy. I was no longer pumped up with enthusiasm. I was no longer anticipating the view, and all my muscles were screaming for me to just get off the mountain.

What I had yet to learn was that finishing a trail takes just as much strength and endurance as starting one. I knew this to be true spiritually because I could say this about everything God has led me to do. All of it has required faith at the beginning, in the middle, and all the way through to the finish.

I bet you could say the same. How many times have you started out strong, believing God for a loved one to be saved, or for a business idea to take off, or for a promotion to come, only to feel your faith fade as time went on? Those moments in any faith journey are pivotal times because it's in those moments we move forward or lose ground.

God wants us to have the faith to finish. Can you think of something you've prayed for, were full of faith for, that is now screaming at you to give up? Face forward today and strengthen your faith. You are able to do *all* things through Him who strengthens you.

Father, thank You for the strength to stay strong in faith at the beginning, in the middle, and all the way to the finish. I look to You today, and I risk trusting You once more. I can do all things through You because You strengthen me. In Jesus' name, amen.

PART 2

HIS DEVOTION IS UNFAILING

The woods are lovely, dark, and deep,
But I have promises to keep,
And miles to go before I sleep,
And miles to go before I sleep.

ROBERT FROST

26 MEMORIAL STONES

This will be a sign among you. In the future, when your children ask you, "What do these stones mean to you?" you should tell them, "The water of the Jordan was cut off in front of the ark of the Lord's covenant. When it crossed the Jordan, the Jordan's water was cut off." Therefore these stones will always be a memorial for the Israelites.

JOSHUA 4:6–7

After the entire nation of Israel had finished crossing the Jordan River, the Lord spoke to Joshua telling him to choose one man from each of the twelve tribes to go pick up a stone from the middle of the Jordan River where the priests were standing. The priests had been standing in the middle of the riverbed, holding the ark of the covenant while everyone crossed over. Once the men each had a stone, they were to carry them and set them down where they would spend the night. The purpose is explained in today's verses. They were to be memorial stones—stones of remembrance of how God backed up the water upstream and provided safe passage. They were stones of remembrance of how God made the impossible possible.

Do you have any memorial stones? I feel sure we both do. Like the children of Israel's, my life of following God has been a faith journey where God has made the impossible possible time and again. The God who brought me through one season is the same God who took me through the next. The God who was with me on the mountaintops was with me in my darkest, deepest valleys. Over and over, I have seen God prove Himself faithful.

And when I find myself facing yet another impossible situation, when I know I will have to endure once more, I pick up my memorial stones. I remember. And I feel the faithfulness of God. I remember how in even my most difficult days and fieriest trials, my God never left me. He brought me through and made a way where there seemed to be no way. Each time I remember, I feel faith rise up in me so I can keep moving forward full of strength and vitality.

What about you? Are you facing the impossible? Are you anxious about something? If you are, it's a good day to pick up some memorial stones and start remembering how God has been faithful in the past, so you can keep living by faith in the present and the future. Write what God has done. List your memorial stones, and thank God for how faithful He has been.

Heavenly Father, thank You for all the times You came through for me. For all the times You provided answers, healing, resources, ideas, and solutions. You are faithful to me. In Jesus' name, amen.

27 YES AND AMEN

Every one of God's promises is "Yes" in him. Therefore, through him we also say "Amen" to the glory of God.

2 CORINTHIANS 1:20

The Bible is a book of promises.[11] And from what Paul wrote to the Corinthians, no matter how many promises God has made, they are all "yes" in Christ. That means what He has promised us in Scripture, He will be faithful to do.

God has promised in His Word that He will never fail. He will never leave us.[12] He will never forsake us (ESV).[13] He has promised that if we trust Him, He will take care of the broken pieces of our lives.[14] He will weave together the good and the bad and work all of it for our good and for His glory.[15] He has promised us salvation, healing, and deliverance.[16] He has promised us faith, hope, and love.[17] He has promised us forgiveness, reconciliation, and restoration.[18]

I know because I've read His promises—and if it's in the Bible and God wants me to have it, then I want it. I've written His promises in journals and on sticky notes. I've memorized them. I've prayed them back to God. Yes! I've reminded Him of His own promises. I've spoken them aloud to myself. Why would I do any of this? To activate my faith in His promises. Imagine that God made you a promise, but you didn't know because you never found it, and therefore you never reminded Him of it.

Have you ever scoured God's Word for a promise to speak in prayer? When I pray about things, I talk to God just like I would talk to you, and in the course of our conversation, I often quote a verse or verses to remind Him of His promises to me. What I have to say on my own matters deeply to God, but when I remind Him of what He has promised me as a follower of Jesus, it activates my faith. And it puts God in remembrance of His Word.

What do you need today? Grace? Mercy? Hope? Faith? Endurance? Go to His Word and find His promise to you for what you need. Write that promise here in the margin of this page. Write it in your heart and mind, figuratively speaking. Then pray God's promise to Him. Say it to yourself. And trust Him that all His promises are yes and amen in Jesus.

Father, thank You for always keeping Your promises, for being so devoted to me. Illuminate Your Word to me today so I can pray it to You and say it to myself. I trust You. In Jesus' name, amen.

28 GOD IS WITH YOU

Be strong and courageous; don't be terrified or afraid of them. For the LORD your God is the one who will go with you; he will not leave you or abandon you.

DEUTERONOMY 31:6

O f all the promises in the Bible, I believe this is the greatest—because when you're in a storm, when you're in the dark, when everything you've leaned on and relied on is being shaken or taken away and you don't know what the future holds, the one thing you can cling to is the promise of God's presence. He never leaves us. He never abandons us. He's always with us. In fact, He is with you right now, wherever you are.

Maybe you're in a season when you feel you have no idea what your next step needs to be, when you have no idea what tomorrow holds. Maybe you feel so alone and don't think you can endure any more. Maybe you've lost the security of your income or the assurance of your health. Maybe you've lost your marriage. Maybe you've had a child walk away— from God, from you, from your family. Let me remind you of the greatest promise: God is with you.

Sometimes, when we're in a dark season, we think the greatest promise from God is the one that will secure what we need or want the most, whether it's something physical, like provisions for our families, or it's more of a relational restoration, or it's the healing we need for our bodies. All of those are important and good, and He wants us standing on His Word for all our needs. But when we're in a night season, and it feels as though no one is standing with us, the greatest promise to hold on to is that our God is with us.

If you're in a season like that right now, focus on the One who is with you. Even if you don't feel Him, trust His promise that He is with you. Even if you can't trace Him, trust His promise that He is with you. This is how we walk by faith and not by sight. We trust He is with us. That He is fully devoted to us. I understand that it's easier to focus on what you're without, but that will make you forget who you're with—and you are with God, who is absolutely faithful to you. He cannot and will not ever leave you or abandon you.

Whatever you're facing, heed the words Moses spoke: "Be strong and courageous. Don't be terrified or afraid. . . . For the LORD your God is the one who will go with you."

Heavenly Father, thank You for Your "withness." Thank You for being with me every step of the way. For never leaving me nor abandoning me. I focus on You now, the One who is with me. In Jesus' name, amen.

29 GOD IS FAITHFUL

By faith even Sarah herself, when she was unable to have children, received power to conceive offspring, even though she was past the age, since she considered that the one who had promised was faithful.

HEBREWS 11:11

Abraham and Sarah longed for a child. Early in their marriage, when they were younger and having a child seemed a reasonable possibility, it didn't happen. When Sarah was sixty-five, God promised her husband Abraham that his descendants would be as numerous as the stars. But even more years passed without them conceiving a child.

The Bible says that Abraham never wavered in his faith, but Sarah struggled to believe that God would deliver on His promise. I don't know about you, but in the face of something so physically impossible, I can understand why Sarah would have struggled to believe having a child was possible. After all, even the Word points out that she was "past the age."

As the story goes, rather than continue to wait on God, Sarah took matters into her own hands. At her suggestion, her servant Hagar gave Abraham a son.

Then, thirteen years later, when the unexpected couldn't and shouldn't have happened, it happened. It had been twenty-five years since God promised Abraham that his descendants would be as numerous as the stars—but twenty-five years later, Sarah conceived and had a son named Isaac. She was ninety years old!

How did this happen? "By faith," the writer of Hebrews tells us. "By faith" Sarah received power to conceive when she was well beyond childbearing because she "considered that the one who had promised was faithful."

It wasn't because her body was fertile, her husband was powerful, or her circumstances were favorable. It wasn't because of breakthroughs in medical science. It was because she grew in her faith that God was faithful—and she quit trying to control the how, the why, and the when.

Until our trust in the Lord eclipses our belief in the limitations of our circumstances, we will not be able to birth the promise God gives us. There is a purpose to the waiting season, to the years when we're wondering if God has heard our prayers. That is when God is strengthening our womb of faith so we can conceive and carry the promise to full term—and then raise it to maturity. God doesn't want us to miscarry the promise, so He prepares us. For Sarah, it took twenty-five years, but she finally considered God accurately—as faithful—despite her age and circumstances.

What is it that God has promised you? Dare to consider Him faithful today.

Heavenly Father, You are faithful! I trust You. And I patiently trust Your timing. I know You've heard me, and while I wait, I will consider You faithful. In Jesus' name, amen.

30 POSSESS WHAT'S YOURS

"See, I have set the land before you. Enter and take possession of the land the LORD *swore to give to your ancestors Abraham, Isaac, and Jacob and their future descendants."*

DEUTERONOMY 1:8

Long before the children of Israel ever made it to the promised land, God set it before them, meaning He gave it to them. It was theirs long before they ever arrived. And yet, even though He gave it to them, they still had to make the journey and possess the land. They first had to complete their journey through the wilderness. Next they had to cross the Jordan River, and then do whatever it took to take possession of all that God had given them. They had to march around the walls surrounding the city of Jericho and see them fall. They had to face giants and defeat them. They had to drive out the inhabitants of the land. In other words, though God gave them what He had promised, they had a part to play to fully receive what was already theirs.

God's promises to us are just the same today. Whatever He has promised us in His Word is already ours, but we have a part to play to fully receive all He's given to us. If we don't do our part, we might find ourselves living with far less than we want and with far less than He wants for us.

God wants us walking in all His goodness. He wants us resting in His peace, feeling wrapped in His love, filled with His hope, and covered in His protection. But if we feel undeserving of all He's already given to us, we may be living a life He never planned for us. Maybe you've embraced a lie from the Enemy—not intentionally, necessarily—and you believe you've messed up so badly God can't come through for you. Nothing could be further from the truth. We all have the same access to the same promises from the same God.

No matter what is in your past, God has an awesome purpose, plan, and future for you. He wants you walking in it all now, but to do that, you'll have to do your part. You'll have to go in and possess the land He's set before you. You'll have to go to His Word and find His promises and possess them for yourself. You'll have to risk believing God. Risk believing His Word. And risk trusting Him. Let's do it together. It is one of the ways we can endure and be faithful to God, who is faithful to us.

Father, thank You for the land You have set before me. For the promises You have made to me in Your Word. I risk believing You, believing Your Word, and trusting You to help me possess what's already mine. In Jesus' name, amen.

31 NO CROSSED FINGERS

God is not a man, that he might lie, or a son of man, that he might change his mind. Does he speak and not act, or promise and not fulfill?

NUMBERS 23:19

When my youngest daughter, Sophia, first started school, she picked up a little trick from her classmates. It took a few times of her doing it before I caught on, but I began to notice that when I would ask her about something, like if she had picked up her toys or not, she'd put her hand behind her back and say, "Yes."

It crossed my mind that it was odd, but she was always an inventive and creative child, so I didn't think much about it until one day when I asked her to pick up her toys, I later walked past her bedroom and noticed them all still in the floor. Not one was in the toy bin.

"Sophia," I called to her, "why did you tell me you picked up all the toys when clearly you haven't? Why did you lie to me?"

"Oh, I didn't lie, Mummy," she'd said, "because I crossed my fingers behind my back. It doesn't count when you cross your fingers."

I immediately realized that's what she'd been doing when she put her hand behind her back. Maybe you had a little one do the same thing. If so, I imagine you probably had to explain all the same lessons I did about telling the truth, and how crossed fingers don't cause a lie not to count.

I remember in all my explaining I told Sophia that God doesn't lie. That God can't lie. And that's part of the reason we're not to lie.

And yet, as she would eventually learn, unlike God, people can lie. They can betray us and break their promises, sometimes leaving us devastated.

I'm so glad God is not one of us and that He can't lie. That He won't lie. Still, I understand that when someone hurts us, when someone breaks their promises to us and our trust is undermined, we can find ourselves unsure if we can trust God—all because we are unsure if we can trust people. We can find ourselves in a place where we stop believing God because we stop believing people.

Let me reassure you: God's Word and all that He promises us in His Word are rock-solid, unequivocal commitments made by God Himself—and God keeps His word. What has He promised you? What has He illuminated in His Word to you? He is faithful to keep His promises, so keep believing. Keep enduring in your faith knowing that He is not a man, that He should lie.

Heavenly Father, help me trust You more. Help me remember that You are faithful, and You will keep Your Word and all Your promises to me. In Jesus' name, amen.

32 HOW ARE YOU WAITING?

Do you not know? Have you not heard? The LORD is the everlasting God, the Creator of the whole earth. He never becomes faint or weary; there is no limit to his understanding. He gives strength to the faint and strengthens the powerless. Youths may become faint and weary, and young men stumble and fall, but those who trust in the LORD will renew their strength; they will soar on wings like eagles; they will run and not become weary, they will walk and not faint.

ISAIAH 40:28–31

H ave you ever felt as though you were in the big waiting season? It's that season when we can grow weary in our faith, when we don't think we can endure one more day of hoping and believing. It seems that as much as we strain to see over the horizon, to get a glimpse of resolve, there's no end in sight.

Maybe you've felt it when you were sick and desperately wanted to be well.

Maybe you've felt it when you prayed for a spouse and longed to be married.

Maybe you've felt it when you saved all the money you could and wanted to buy a house.

In every one of my big waiting seasons, it's been good to know that no matter how weary or tired or faint I might feel, God never feels that way. Instead, He gives power to the faint. When we put our trust in Him, He increases our strength.

Another translation of today's verse says that those who *wait* upon the Lord will renew their strength.[19] Waiting and trusting are much the same—and neither of them is passive. When we wait upon the Lord, it's not a time when we go sit on the couch and eat chips and salsa and just wait for something to happen. It's much more active. It's a mind-set that engages our faith. It's a waiting based on anticipation. It's an outlook on life that says, "I might not know what the future holds, but I know the God who holds the future." It's a faith that believes, *He is good, and because He is good, even if I can't trace Him in this current moment, I can trust Him.*

How are you waiting? Are you waiting with expectancy? Or with dread, fear, or a sense of despair? Look to God, who gives us strength. Who gives us power. Who gives us might through the anointing of the Holy Spirit to be able to not only get through our big waiting season but to thrive in the midst of it. Refocus your faith today and determine to go through this season with a sense of life, a sense of vitality, a sense of knowing that God has your future in His hands.

Heavenly Father, I anticipate the future with faith, with energy, with renewed strength and passion. I trust You, even when I can't trace You. I put my hopes and dreams in Your hands. In Jesus' name, amen.

33 MORE POWERFUL
THAN A STORM

Last night an angel of the God I belong to and serve stood by me and said,
"Don't be afraid, Paul. It is necessary for you to appear before Caesar. And
indeed, God has graciously given you all those who are sailing with you."
ACTS 27:23–24

W hen Paul said the words in today's scripture, he was a prisoner on a ship headed for Rome, and they were in the middle of a storm. The sky was pitch-black and they could not see which way to navigate. No moon, no stars, nothing to guide the captain. From all the indicators, it looked like they were surely going to die.

But Paul had a promise. An angel had told Paul what God wanted: for him to stand before Caesar. Why? Because if Paul could get to Rome, he could testify of the goodness of God and the gospel would go out from the greatest city on earth at the time. There was far more at stake than just Paul. There was the future of multitudes.

When you have a promise from God, it doesn't matter what size storm you're in or how dark the night is. There is not a demon in hell or a person on earth who can hold you back from the plans of God for your life. That doesn't mean you will not be tossed by the winds and waves, and even feel nauseated at times. It might feel like the storm is going to take you out, but it won't, because in the storm you are building strength, endurance, and tenacity.

Do you have a promise? Have you been holding on to something based in the Word of God?

There have been times when Nick and I have been in a storm, and we've reviewed every promise God has given to us. We have reminded God of what He's promised our children. What He's promised to do in our ministry and through the work of A21. Lives are at stake, far more than just ours.

I have learned that the promises of God will always be more powerful than any storm. So I'll ask you again: Do you have a promise? What is it that you're holding on to, that's been written in your journal or Bible for a long, long time? Hold it up to God once more. Let Him know that you will be as faithful to Him as He's been to you. Let Him know that you will endure in faith until you see the promise.

Paul did, and he got to Rome. He testified before Caesar. And the message of the gospel went forth. God's promise to him came to pass, and God's promise to you will too.

Heavenly Father, I thank You that Your promise is more powerful than any storm I may find myself in. I'm holding on to Your promises for my life. I know that what You've promised will come to pass. In Jesus' name, amen.

34 DON'T JUMP SHIP

Some sailors tried to escape from the ship; they had let down the skiff into the sea, pretending that they were going to put out anchors from the bow. Paul said to the centurion and the soldiers, "Unless these men stay in the ship, you cannot be saved." Then the soldiers cut the ropes holding the skiff and let it drop away.

ACTS 27:30–32

In the middle of a storm, the sailors on the ship carrying Paul to Rome tried to jump ship. They were fearful and schemed how they could get to shore. They knew the ship was going to run aground, and they did not want to be on a ship that was going to be destroyed by the rocks.

But according to Paul, there was only one way for the men on the ship to live—they had to stay on board. Paul told the centurion and the soldiers that the men had to stay in the ship to be saved because that's what the angel from the Lord had told him. The provision and protection of God for all the men on that ship—all 276 of them—was the promise from God.

I don't know what you're facing, but let this verse encourage you. Don't jump ship in your relationship with Jesus. I know you could be in a place of feeling bone-tired. I know you could be more disappointed than you've ever been. The fear you might be facing is real. Your defenses may be down, and you might be feeling very fragile. Your emotions may feel raw. Hold on to whatever Jesus has told you. Hold on to who He is and to who you are in Him. Hold on to all He's promised you in His Word. Remember that He is faithful—even when people might not be.

Stay faithful and connected to Jesus the way He is faithful and connected to you. From today's passage, I understand as well that sometimes, though it makes no sense to us, the ship has to run aground—and the ship can be anything in our lives. When that happens, we usually don't understand why or how, and it's in those moments we have to trust that God is still in control. That His promises will prevail. Even when all looks lost.

Keep your eyes on Jesus. Hold on to your promise. Paul did, and everyone lived. The ship did run aground. The waves pounded it, and it did break apart. Those who could swim did. Those who couldn't held on to planks and whatever would float. But God was faithful, and everyone safely reached the shore.

You will too. Keep enduring. Keep holding on. Keep being faithful to the One who is faithful to you.

Heavenly Father, I will not jump ship. I will stay on board. I will endure in faith. I will hold on to the promise You have given me. In Jesus' name, amen.

35 PREPARE FOR
WHAT'S NEXT

When it was about daylight, Paul urged them all to take food, saying, "Today is the fourteenth day that you have been waiting and going without food, having eaten nothing. So I urge you to take some food. For this is for your survival, since none of you will lose a hair from your head."

ACTS 27:33–34

When I read today's verse, I can't help but think of how natural and practical Paul's instructions were. The men on the ship with him hadn't eaten in fourteen days. They were about to run aground and were going to have to swim ashore. To make it they would need strength. They would need to eat.

Sometimes the answers we need are actually quite simple. Yes, they always involve the spiritual, but typically they involve very natural and practical steps too.

When I first thought about climbing mountains in Southern California, I knew I wasn't able to do it physically; though spiritually I knew it was something God wanted me to do. My level of fitness was good, but it wasn't good enough to sustain climbing for as long as eight hours. Mentally, as I began to grasp what would be required of me, I knew I needed to get my head in the right space and increase my capacity to endure physically too. So I ate more nutritiously. I physically built more strength, stamina, and endurance in the gym. I got adequate sleep. I focused my mind by watching videos of all things to do with conquering mountains. I even watched a movie where a two-man team scaled three thousand feet of a solid granite wall in Yosemite National Park in California called the Dawn Wall. I couldn't help but cry when they finally made it. They were the first to do it, and watching them made me want to be next. I know—sometimes I'm a little too zealous. But everything I did prepared me so I could endure the hikes my friend Dawn planned for us.

Maybe you know what God wants you to do next. You've prayed about it and prepared for it spiritually. Now is the time to ensure you are ready for it physically, because God's faithfulness to us includes every aspect of our lives, not just our spiritual well-being. He didn't just want to save Paul and the others from the storm they were in; He wanted them to be strong for what would come next. They were going to have to swim ashore. So he told them to eat. Something so simple. So practical.

What is God showing you to do to prepare physically for what's next? Whatever it is, do it, because doing both the spiritual and the natural thing is what will get you there.

Heavenly Father, thank You for being so practical and for caring so deeply about every aspect of my life. Show me what I'm to do next, and I will do it. In Jesus' name, amen.

36 WHO IS YOUR SHEPHERD?

"I am the good shepherd. The good shepherd lays down his life for the sheep."
JOHN 10:11

'm not a farm girl, but I did grow up in Australia, and there are plenty of sheep there. So while I don't think I'd be of any help on a farm, I am familiar enough with sheep to be intrigued that Jesus calls us sheep and Himself our Good Shepherd.

From what I do know about sheep, they need more protection and care than most other livestock because they're defenseless and needy. They can't run fast because they have little legs. They don't have sharp teeth to fight off predators. They're easily frightened. Why then would God describe us as sheep and Himself as our Shepherd, not once or twice, but more than two hundred times in the Bible?

Perhaps it's because we, like sheep, need a whole lot of protection. Every one of us, somewhere along our journey, needs to know that Jesus is there, that Jesus cares, that Jesus is protecting us, that Jesus has our back in every way. It's one more way we will endure in our journey of faith. I think that no matter who we are, wherever we are in life, no matter how long we have been following Jesus, even if we're some kind of shepherd ourselves—at home, at work, or in ministry—we are still sheep that need a Shepherd.

When we get too close to the edge of something, we need Him to pull us back to safety. When we lose sight of where we're going and wander away, we need Him to come find us and bring us home. When we are distracted and have no idea what the Enemy is planning, we need Jesus to intervene. It seems that no matter how smart we are, how intelligent we are, how articulate we are, how connected we are, how resourced we are, we still need the Good Shepherd. We still need Jesus.

It's so easy to reach out and make other things our shepherd. To put our trust in our resources of time, talents, gifts, and abilities. To put our trust in our loved ones. When we put our sense of significance or security, of protection, affirmation, or strength in anything or anyone outside of Jesus, we will find ourselves wandering where we never wanted to be. Like sheep who need a shepherd to look after us once more.

Renew your relationship with Jesus as the Good Shepherd today. Think of all the ways He protects you, is faithful to you, and looks out for you. Even when you aren't aware. Declare your dependence on Him and thank Him for His faithfulness.

Jesus, thank You for being the Good Shepherd to me. Thank You for protecting me, especially when I have no idea I'm even in danger Thank You for being faithful to me. In Your name I pray, amen.

37 LIGHT IN THE VALLEY

Even when I go through the darkest valley, I fear no danger, for you are with me; your rod and your staff—they comfort me.

PSALM 23:4

D avid, a man after God's own heart, spent many years being chased by his enemies. I imagine he often wondered when the promise of him becoming king would be realized. He had to endure trial after trial and repeated attempts on his life, and yet he had built such trust and confidence in God that he said he would not fear in the darkest valley. That he would not fear any danger, that he trusted God was with him. What an incredible indication of how having to endure constant adversity built implicit trust.

When I look at my own life, I think of David. It seems there's a kind of faith that comes only from going through the dark valleys. It would be wonderful to have nothing but mountaintop experiences, but after more than thirty years of following Jesus, I have found the journey to include plenty of dark valleys. I've been through a lot of challenges. A lot of attacks. I've made mistakes and had failures that I've had to apologize for and move on from, but through it all, God has always been with me, just as He was with David.

The Enemy will never stop trying to take us out, to make us want to stop, to make us want to give up. He is relentless. But so is God. He is relentless in His love, His goodness, His faithfulness to us, and His presence with us.

More than once, when I've been walking through a valley, I've looked up and shouted to God and to myself words like, "I'm walking through the valley. I can't see You, God. I can't feel You. I can't sense You. But I trust You are there. I know You're going to help me find You in the midst of all I'm going through." Just saying something like this helps me to endure by reminding me that He is with me. Just as He's with you. Always. He never leaves us. Not even when we can't see Him or feel Him or sense Him. He's still there.

If you sense in your mind the absence of God, then challenge your thinking. If you have to, shout like I have. Declare the truth of His presence. He is with you.

Heavenly Father, thank You that You are with me. Always. Even in the dark. Thank You for lighting up the dark valleys and showing me the way forward. In Jesus' name, amen.

38 HE IS FAITHFUL

Let us hold on to the confession of our hope without wavering, since he who promised is faithful.

HEBREWS 10:23

On my fiftieth birthday, Nick threw a surprise party for me that included lots of food, friends, cake, and dancing Zorba the Greek on a boat in Southern California. We had an amazing night of fun. As I got off the boat and said goodbye to my friends, I checked my phone . . . and there were twenty-six missed calls from my brother Andrew in Australia telling me that our mum had passed away.

It was like the best of times and the worst of times all happening at once. Here I was, all ready to reflect on the night and soak up all the happiness, and instead, I rode home heartbroken and in shock. My mum was older and hadn't been in perfect health for a while, but all our family felt confident that we had more time. To me, it just didn't make sense.

Have you ever been in such a place? I'm not sure there are any of us who haven't found ourselves at some stage in life trying to make sense of what just doesn't make sense. I can't be the only one who has asked God, "Why did this happen? Where were You in the midst of it all? Why, God, why?"

We don't expect sickness, do we? We don't expect breakups. We don't expect to lose our jobs or our homes or those we love, especially when it's way too soon. We don't expect to lose what we think we're not supposed to lose. But we do sometimes. And in those moments, it's all too easy to question God and His goodness.

To strengthen our faith, to endure when we aren't sure how, we need to remind ourselves that He who promised is faithful. I understand that there are times when we trust God because of what we can see, but there are also times when we have to trust God in spite of what we see. Those are the times we need to remind ourselves of who God is and what we know to be true about Him.

God is good. God does good. God is holy. God is just. God is love. God is full of grace and mercy. God is kind and forgiving. God knows all things. God does not make mistakes. God is in control.

We have to remind ourselves that we are not the one person God will not be faithful to. It's just not possible. That's not His character or His nature. No, things won't always go the way we want; in fact, most likely they won't. But that doesn't change who He is. He who has promised is faithful.

Heavenly Father, thank You for being faithful to me, even when everything seems so unsure. I put my trust in You, in spite of what I see. Thank You for Your faithfulness to me. In Jesus' name, amen.

39 CELEBRATE HIM

Though the fig tree does not bud and there is no fruit on the vines, though the olive crop fails and the fields produce no food, though the flocks disappear from the pen and there are no herds in the stalls, yet I will celebrate in the LORD; I will rejoice in the God of my salvation!

HABAKKUK 3:17–18

When Habakkuk walked this earth, he lived in confusing times, and he didn't hold back in telling God how he felt about it. His book is a mixture of his addresses to a gracious God and God's replies to a gracious soul.

As he worked through his frustrations, in the span of just three chapters, he went from a place of great perplexity to where he just couldn't work out what was going on in his nation and why God was doing what He was doing, to declaring a faith so strong it says that though everything may fail to produce—the fig tree, the vines, the olive crop, the flocks, the herds . . . everything that yielded fruit in his life—"Yet I will celebrate in the Lord; I will rejoice in the God of my salvation."

His name means "to embrace, to wrestle with," and that's what he did.[20] He wrestled with God, and because he did, he went from being gripped by fear to being filled with faith, from perplexity to praise, from tears to triumph, from worry to worship, from confusion to confidence. He endured and landed in a place of faith in God and faithfulness to God.

When was the last time you felt anxious about what's happening in the world? No doubt, like Habakkuk, we live in confusing times. Every day there are reasons to feel concern. But when we grow anxious, we can't stay in that place. We need to wrestle with God so we can keep enduring, so we can land in a place that's faithful and faith-filled.

To keep myself in a place of strong faith, I take all my concerns to God. I tell Him when I feel anxious or fearful. Then, in my own words, I declare to Him what Habakkuk did: "Though the fig tree does not bud . . . though nothing goes the way I hope or imagine . . . though nothing appears fruitful . . . yet I will trust You. I will celebrate You. I will rejoice in the God of my salvation!"

Are the times we're living in giving you reason for concern? Do you feel your heart growing anxious? Do like Habakkuk did and wrestle. Take your concerns to God and then make a declaration today that no matter what, you will put your trust in God. You will trust in His faithfulness. You will rejoice in the God of your salvation!

Heavenly Father, thank You that You are always faithful to me, regardless of what goes on in this world and in my world. I place all my trust in You. I celebrate you. I rejoice in You, the God of my salvation! In Jesus' name, amen.

40 PICK THE GOOD FIGHT

Fight the good fight of the faith. Take hold of eternal life to which you were called and about which you have made a good confession in the presence of many witnesses.

1 TIMOTHY 6:12

When my Sophia was growing up, I could never get her to eat fruit. Not apples. Not oranges. Not grapes. I tried everything. I remember trying to sneak fruit into dishes I baked in hopes she wouldn't notice, but I think she somehow had this built-in fruit detector, and my attempts rarely worked. Getting her to eat fruit, to at least try a small piece, became a fight I had to walk away from, even though I knew for her health's sake, she needed to eat it.

Maybe one of your kids was like that. Perhaps what you fought over was broccoli or brussels sprouts. Take it from me; they will survive. Don't lose sleep over it. It's not worth the fight.

As simple as it sounds, some fights are worth it—and some are not. It's critical that we learn which fights to fight and which ones to walk away from. Our kids not eating a piece of fruit or a serving of vegetables is a fight to walk away from. Being frustrated with your husband over leaving the toilet seat up again is a fight to walk away from. I have come to understand that until Jesus comes back and splits the eastern sky, it's possible that I might find the toilet seat in the up position in our house, so when I do, I don't need to fight that fight. I just need to walk away.

The reason is that there is a fight worth having. There is a fight worth throwing all our energy and emotion into. There is a fight that's crucial to every aspect of our lives. It's the good fight of faith. And at the end of the day, that's the fight the Enemy is after because he knows if you don't have your faith, he has the power to take you out.

What fights are you fighting? If we are going to endure to the end, we cannot jump into every fight. We cannot prematurely expend all our energy. We must save our strength for the right battles. Maybe it's time to let some of the fights go. The one with your kids. The one with your spouse. The one with your boss. The one with the difficult coworker. The one with yourself. If you're going to endure in this lifetime walking by faith, triumphant in your faith, then pick the best fight. Fight the good fight of faith.

Father, thank You for showing me how to walk away from all the fights I'm wasting my strength on and show me how to fight the good fight of faith. Show me how to endure living by faith. In Jesus' name, amen.

41 WE'RE ALL CALLED

May the God of peace himself sanctify you completely. And may your whole spirit, soul, and body be kept sound and blameless at the coming of our Lord Jesus Christ. He who calls you is faithful; he will do it.

1 THESSALONIANS 5:23–24

We're all called to fulfill a purpose, to be all that God created us to be and to do all that God created us to do. Our calling is that God-given passion that can never be quenched, that assignment we were born to fulfill.

Part of my calling is to share the gospel and to see people come to Christ. I'm called to lead and teach others to lead so they can learn how to be full of the power of God, so they can fulfill what God has called them to do. I'm called to be a wife and a mother. A friend. And I'm called to help abolish slavery everywhere, forever.

These callings are my assignments, my vocations. The word *vocation* is from the Latin *vocatio*, which means "calling." At its core, work is a calling, designed by God to fulfill a purpose that is outside of oneself, a purpose that brings glory to God and blesses others.[21]

As I have answered every calling, I have always felt unqualified. At this stage of my life, I've come to think that's part of God's plan. Our willingness to push forward and risk trusting Him is part of how we grow our faith and build endurance. It's how we trust in Him, and not in ourselves.

Whether our calling is to start a business, launch an outreach, or walk across the street to meet a new neighbor, when God's Spirit gently nudges us to make a bold step, take a risk, serve others, save a life, or commit, we rarely feel ready. But feeling ready isn't what it's about. It's about stepping out in faith and doing what God's called us to do, trusting Him through it all.

Have you identified what God has called you to do? If you are reading this, it means you are still alive, and God has not left you on the planet to do nothing. He wants us to bear fruit. This is why we need endurance. I imagine we'll always think we lack the courage, the strength, the wisdom, the money, the influence, the experience, the education, the organization, and the backing, but it isn't about what we have or don't have. It's about who He is. And according to what Paul wrote to the Thessalonians, He who calls us is faithful. So let's be faithful to Him. Let's do all that He's called us to do.

Heavenly Father, thank You for being faithful to call me and to help me fulfill all that You've called me to do. Use me in every way You want. In Jesus' name, amen.

42 PASS THE TEST

For you, God, tested us; you refined us as silver is refined.
PSALM 66:10

For a few years, I was in grad school at Wheaton College, working on my master's degree in evangelism and leadership. For four years, I attended lectures, researched and wrote papers, read books, and took loads of tests. Of all that I did, tests were my least favorite. And to be completely transparent, as much as I love learning, I prefer cutting up in the back of the classroom to doing any schoolwork. But to get my master's, I had to do the work. And take all the tests.

For every test I took, I did my best to study and be prepared. I did not want to take any test a second time. I didn't want to fail any of the tests. I wanted to get good grades and move to the next level.

Do you remember what it was like to be in school and take tests? Maybe you're in school right now and, like me, tests are your least favorite part. Well, I have news for us all. Even after we're long out of school, we'll still be taking tests, because tests are part of our spiritual journey. Not pen-and-paper ones. Not online ones. But real-life ones. Tests that are designed by God to stretch our faith and build our endurance. Tests that refine us and make us stronger.

Think back to the last time you took a test in school. Did you ever notice that while you were taking your exam, the teacher rarely spoke, other than to tell you to use a number 2 pencil and to keep your eyes on your own paper, of course? The teacher is always silent during a test because he or she wants to see how you're going to pass the test.

In similar fashion, sometimes I think we're expecting God to speak to us in the middle of our tests, but He takes the position of the teacher. It's as though He says, "I'm being silent because I'm going to see what's on the inside of you."

We can get so frustrated in those times, can't we? We want Him to talk, but it often feels as if we are met with silence.

The best way to pass every test is to remain faithful as He is faithful. To endure and to keep moving forward, with our eyes on Him.

Father, help me pass every test, to keep my eyes on You, and to not be concerned when You grow silent. You are still there and still faithful. You're just wanting me to pass the test. In Jesus' name, amen.

43 MUM'S WALL

By faith the walls of Jericho fell down after being marched around by the Israelites for seven days.

HEBREWS 11:30

B y faith the walls of Jericho fell down, but only after the Israelites obeyed God's instructions and did exactly as God said. I imagine marching around a wall for seven days must have made no sense at all to them. And yet they obeyed God.

Have you ever felt God wanting you to do something that made no sense to you? And yet you obeyed, took a step of faith, and it all worked out? I have, and it wasn't easy—and since then I've learned it rarely is easy, but it's always worth it.

When I first became a fully devoted follower of Jesus, it caused great tension in my home. My family felt I had joined some kind of cult, because they could not fathom anyone would be so on fire for Jesus twenty-four hours a day. Admittedly, I lacked wisdom in my newfound zeal, and a deep chasm formed between my mum and me. There was a period when she barely spoke to me because she felt so betrayed, so fearful that I had abandoned my cultural heritage. It was painful to live in the same house and be ignored.

At one point, I felt God giving me instructions that I thought were strange. I was to sit in our living room every Tuesday evening and watch

Mum's favorite soap opera with her—while making no sarcastic remarks about the dramatic acting or predictable plot twists. Can you tell I wasn't a fan? I'd like to think I'm just given to much deeper story lines, but God knows everything, and back then He knew I'd be tempted to critique every scene. I'm much more well behaved now. I promise. Anyway, after watching TV with her, I was to make her coffee and wash up the dishes in the sink.

It sounds so simple, but it was unbelievably hard. For almost a year, I sat and watched. In silence. When I offered her coffee, she wouldn't answer me. So many times, I would go into the kitchen with tears streaming down my face and wash the dishes, put them away, and go to bed. I'd lie in bed and cry myself to sleep. But one day, after about nine months, I asked if she wanted coffee and she nodded her head. Just as it happened for the children of Israel on that seventh lap, I saw Mum's wall start to tumble. It wasn't long until our whole relationship turned around and became better than it had ever been.

What has God moved you in your heart to do? Go ahead and do it. Endure in your faith for as long as it takes, trusting Him that the walls will come tumbling down.

Father, thank You that no walls are too fortified for You to take down. Whatever You show me to do, I will do by faith. In Jesus' name, amen.

44 QUITE THE OPPOSITE

You are good, and you do what is good; teach me your statutes.

PSALM 119:68

When I was growing up, particularly when I'd get out of line, I would hear my parents or one of my aunts or uncles say to me, "Christine, don't do that or God will punish you." Their words of caution were desperate attempts to control me because I could be quite a stinker. I understand they didn't mean any real harm, but through the years their words forged an image of God in my mind that was all wrong. I saw Him as this big guy in the sky with a huge stick who was poised to thump me on the head. I saw Him just waiting for me to do something wrong, and because I did a lot wrong, I was forever thinking He was going to punish me.

Somehow, in my head, I saw Him as old and boring and someone who never wanted to have any fun. Certainly not as someone I would ever want to spend time with or talk to or someone I would ever feel any love from. The way I grew up, the last thing I would have ever believed about God was what David wrote: "You are good, and you do what is good."

Can you imagine all the undoing that had to happen in my life when I became a follower of Christ? I certainly could never have endured faith-filled and hope-filled this long if I hadn't changed my perspective of Him.

What is your perception of God? How do you see Him? Sometimes, when circumstances in our lives haven't gone the best way, we can develop a perception that God is angry or depressed or miserable. But God isn't like the people we might have grown up with or been around.

The Bible says He's good and He does good. It says He's loving and joyful. He's full of compassion, kindness, mercy, and peace. It's so important that we see God the way He is and not the way people are, because how we view God determines how we will view and live life.

Are you living as though He's good and does good, or are you living as if He's a big guy in the sky ready to thump you?

What if you started today looking for how God is described in the Bible and then let those descriptions replace the distorted images you might have? Start with Psalm 119:68: He is good and He does good. That's what I did. It took a long time—many years, in fact—but over those years I learned He is nothing like what my family taught me. He is quite the opposite in most every way.

Heavenly Father, show me who You are in Your Word. Help me see You and know You as You are—as someone who is good and who does what is good. In Jesus' name, amen.

45 SHOW HIM YOUR FAITHFULNESS

So that I would not exalt myself, a thorn in the flesh was given to me, a messenger of Satan to torment me so that I would not exalt myself. Concerning this, I pleaded with the Lord three times that it would leave me. But he said to me, "My grace is sufficient for you, for my power is perfected in weakness."

2 CORINTHIANS 12:7–9

More than once in my life, I've asked God to take something away. When I was diagnosed with cancer, I wanted to be delivered from it. But that's not how it worked out. I actually had four separate conditions at the time: a growth on the left side of my throat, nodules on my vocal cords, a throat infection, and thyroid cancer.

When I learned of my diagnosis, I immediately prayed. I leaned into God and drew on His scriptures that told of His healing power. I wanted a miracle.

I can't explain it, but two weeks later, when they ran a second set of tests on my larynx to check the nodules on my vocal cords, my doctor said, "I don't know what happened, but the nodules are gone." There was no need to do surgery to remove them.

Despite this amazing news, the rest of my conditions remained. Why

I received a miracle for the nodules and not for my thyroid or throat, I don't know, but I kept enduring, moving forward in faith, and trusting God with all my heart.

I relied on what God said to Paul when he asked for the thorn in his flesh to leave: "My grace is sufficient for you." Over the next few months, as more tests were run, I had to accept that His grace would be sufficient for me. I had to trust in His faithfulness, despite my circumstances. I had to trust in His character and nature, particularly as I didn't understand His actions. I had to trust Him more than my feelings.

I had surgery three months later and was given the all-clear soon after that. I've never believed my cancer was from God, as I do not believe that God sends sickness, because there is no sickness in heaven or in God Himself. But for some reason, in His sovereignty, He didn't miraculously take it all away. Instead, He allowed me to walk through it. He showed me His faithfulness, and I showed Him mine.

What is it that you've asked Him to take away that He hasn't? Trust in His character and His nature. It will be key to your enduring with faith. Trust that His grace is sufficient for you.

Heavenly Father, thank You for always being faithful to me and for showing me more ways to be faithful to You. Your grace is sufficient for me in all I go through. In Jesus' name, amen.

46 WHEN NOTHING
MAKES SENSE

The righteous one will live by his faith.
HABAKKUK 2:4

The nation of Judah, where Habakkuk lived, had bowed down to immorality, idolatry, materialism, and greed. So he cried out to God and told Him how bad things were, and he asked Him what was going to happen.

God's answer was nothing like what Habakkuk wanted or expected. God told him that a nation even more unrighteous—which turned out to be Babylon—would come and overtake them and rule over them.

As you can imagine, Habakkuk then said pretty much what we would say: "That's not fair."

The rest of Habakkuk's conversation with God makes up the three chapters of this very short book of the Bible. Habakkuk wrestles with God, and he comes to several profound conclusions, including one that is repeated multiple times in the New Testament. He says, "The righteous one will live by his faith."

Like Habakkuk, I don't understand everything that happens in the world. Bad things happen to good people. Things take so much longer than they should. Every day there is something I find unjust and unfair.

But I have learned to never let my conversation with God end there. I keep talking until I come to the same conclusion Habakkuk did. The one Paul did. That the writer of Hebrews did.[22] "The righteous one will live by his faith."

I can't control anything anyway, and neither can you. When God finally promised Habakkuk that He would deal with the Babylonians, He did—seventy years later. I've never waited that long on God. I have never endured in faith that long. I can't even imagine what that would feel like. But I am determined to live as though I would.

I have found that trusting God brings the maturity and the strength we need to step into the plans and purposes God has for us. If we let ourselves stay in a place of saying and believing that what we see and experience and feel is unfair, we won't reach our destiny. Not in the way that God has designed.

So let's trust Him, especially when nothing in our world makes sense. Let's trust Him to get us to where we need to be, mentally, spiritually, emotionally, and physically. Let's be the righteous who live and endure by faith.

Heavenly Father, You know all the things I see and feel are so unfair. You know what I do not understand. But I declare that I will live and endure by faith even when life feels unfair and even when I do not understand. I trust You. In Jesus' name, amen.

47 PAY ATTENTION

For this reason, we must pay attention all the more to what we have heard, so that we will not drift away.

HEBREWS 2:1

P*ay attention* . . . I heard words of warning like this all throughout my childhood. I learned to speak Greek before I spoke English, and my mother always spoke to us in Greek. When she wanted to really get something across to my two brothers and me, she would use the same words as the writer of Hebrews did: *perissoteros prosechein.* When she spoke these words, she was telling us to be careful and pay *extra* attention. Her tone would be urgent, serious, instructive, and commanding of our focus—especially when it was about something critical to our well-being, like when she taught us to look both ways before running after a ball that had rolled into the street. Or when she wanted us to stay put on a bench and be safe while she tended to some business at a bank or in a store.

Perissoteros prosechein.

She said it when we learned to ride our bikes, when we walked to school, or ran across the neighborhood to a friend's house.

Perissoteros prosechein.

"Pay extra attention," my mother said.

"Pay extra attention," the writer of Hebrews said.

Why pay extra attention? *Lest you drift.* It's as though the writer knew the more familiar we became, the less attention we would pay—to God, His Word, and His ways. He knew the more we learned, the more likely we would take it all for granted—and miss the awe of our salvation.

Pay attention. So you don't drift.

Personally, I don't want to miss a thing that God has planned for me. Even when it's easier to be distracted, I want to pay attention. I want to be found faithful. I want to do all that God's called me to do. I want to be all that He's created me to be. I want to endure in my faith every day of my life, until I stand before Him. Isn't that the cry of your heart too?

There is so much we can't change in this world and in our own worlds, but we can reset our focus. Whatever is pulling on your attention—a work situation, a heartache in your family, a loss you never saw coming, maybe bills piling up that you can't pay—things it seems you can do nothing about, do what you can. Turn your eyes on Jesus once more. Look to Him. Put your trust in Him. Show yourself faithful to the One who is eternally faithful to you. In the midst of our praying and believing, this is how we won't drift. It's how we will endure, living by faith.

Heavenly Father, I reset my focus today. I turn my attention to You, and I put my trust in You. I don't want to miss anything You have for me. In Jesus' name, amen.

48 TOO BIG TO MISS

He renews my life; he leads me along the right paths for his name's sake.
PSALM 23:3

One of the things I have pursued fervently all my Christian life is the will of God. I guess I spent enough time out of His will that once I became a fully devoted follower of Jesus, there was nowhere else I wanted to be. Being in the will of God has always been a place of security, comfort, and reassurance for me. Things may not go as planned or expected—they rarely do—but I'm confident that if I'm moving forward in His will, I can have faith that all will be well. I can trust in His goodness. I can be confident in His promise: "He leads me along the right paths."

Have you recently asked God what His will was concerning something? Maybe a job change? A move? What about whether to date someone or not? Better to ask early on than to have to break it off later, right? I remember when Nick and I dated, I was always checking in with the Lord, partly because I wanted so desperately to be in His will, but also because I was so anxious. If only I'd known then how to rest in God and trust Him implicitly. Back then, I wanted everything to be perfect, but that's not reality, is it? Relationships are messy, just like our journey of following God. When Nick asked me to marry him, I was so overwhelmed, I told him I couldn't give him an answer right then, and I ran to the bathroom. Yes, I really did this. I called my best friend, Kylie, and told her I was freaking out. Looking back, it was more about control than anything, but still, I was in the most picturesque place, with the most loving man, being given a beautiful marriage proposal, and all I could do was run to the bathroom and call my best friend. I was so scared of messing it all up and missing the will of God. But that kind of thinking only paralyzes us, and it actually keeps us from moving forward. It keeps us from enduring in our walk of faithfully trusting God.

If you're in a place where you're wondering whether you're in the will of God or not, don't panic. Don't lose sleep over it. Don't become spiritually paralyzed and throw on the brakes, all because you're fearful of missing His will. God is a big God. He's hard to miss. If your heart is for Him, you will find Him. After all, He's promised to lead us along right paths for His name's sake.

Heavenly Father, thank You for leading me along the right paths. Thank You for assuring me that I will not miss You. You really are too big for me to miss. Thank You for being so faithful to me. In Jesus' name, amen.

49 HE'S STILL THERE

"Look, I am with you and will watch over you wherever you go. I will bring you back to this land, for I will not leave you until I have done what I have promised you."

GENESIS 28:15

There are few things I love more than a late-evening stroll on the beach when the sun is setting, especially when I get to enjoy it with Nick. One evening, as we were admiring the orange glow on the ocean near our home, our entire panorama suddenly disappeared. One minute we were looking at breathtaking views, and the next we couldn't see anything. Not the island in the distance where the sun always dropped behind it. Not any boats that were just outlined in front of it. Not even the people we had seen strolling farther up the shoreline.

In the few minutes that we'd been watching, a marine layer had moved in—something that commonly happens on the west coast of the US.[23] Have you ever seen one of those iconic photos of San Francisco's Golden Gate Bridge and the rolling fog underneath? That's a marine layer, and it totally blocks your ability to see anything.

As Nick and I continued to watch, it slowly swallowed everything in sight. Without thinking, I blurted out, "Where's the island? Where did it go?" I'll never forget how Nick answered so matter-of-factly: "It's right where it's always been. You just can't see it. Nothing's changed."

The irony of my question and Nick's answer left me with a perspective of God that I'm still holding on to. How many times have we felt as if we were moving forward spiritually, that we could see far and go the distance, only to have what feels like a marine layer move in and completely cloud our vision? It can happen so easily. One minute we can have great clarity spiritually, and the next we can feel so blindsided by something we never saw coming, left in what feels like a giant bank of fog.

When that happens, it never means that God's moved. It doesn't mean His plans won't prevail or that His provisions won't come. The goal, the direction, the vision, the calling, the objective He's given us—none of that has changed. His purpose for us has not changed. All that's happened is that we just can't see as clearly. How important it is then for us to remain steady. To stay faithful. To keep enduring. And not get rattled by a temporarily obstructed view.

Has a marine layer moved in on you? It doesn't change a thing. He's still there. He's promised, "I am with you and will watch over you wherever you go . . . for I will not leave you until I have done what I have promised you."

Heavenly Father, You always lead me forward, even through the fog. I trust You that You will not leave me until You have done what you have promised. In Jesus' name, amen.

50 FAITHFUL LOVE

Lord, your faithful love reaches to heaven, your faithfulness to the clouds.
PSALM 36:5

When Dawn and I first started hiking together, I had no idea what I was doing. I just knew that when she invited me, it was something I wanted to do.

At the end of each day's hike, when I got home, my legs would feel so useless that I was never quite sure if I'd make it in the house. Nothing felt better right then than soaking in an Epsom salt bath and later resting my legs in a compression massager. I could have sat in the massager all the next week, for sure, but that's not really a good idea. Instead, I always walked the next day, usually along the beach, to move out the soreness. With every hike, I grew stronger and more confident.

Almost a year into our adventures, Dawn led us up Mystic Canyon Trail and down Monroe Truck Trail into the city of Glendora, California. The trail is rated as difficult, with an elevation gain of more than 2,500 feet, so making it to the top was another victory in itself. But for the first time there was a surprise waiting for me at the top.

As we stopped to catch our breath at the summit and take in the sweeping views, Dawn pointed out the peaks of Cucamonga and Ontario. I couldn't help but marvel that I had already climbed both of them. I remembered how difficult it felt, how daunting it was, how there were times I felt as if I would need to be airlifted out! But that never happened. I had actually made it off both mountains alive! I could also see Saddleback Mountain—the mountain with the highest peak in Orange County. The one I had yet to hike.

What a snapshot. In one panoramic sweep I could see where I'd come from and where I had yet to go, and all I could do was thank God for His faithfulness to me.

What has He helped you do that you didn't think you had the strength, the courage, the knowledge, the discipline, or the faith to do? Sometimes, to keep enduring, we need to stop and take in the sweeping views of our lives. We need to remember that it is by His grace and might and strength that we prevailed. Let's take the time today to see how far we've come and then thank Him for what's coming next. It's amazing when we can see how far His love and faithfulness reach, and we realize it's higher than any mountain we could ever climb.

Heavenly Father, thank You for all You've done to bring me this far in my life. And thank You for all that is yet to unfold in the future. Your love is faithful to me. In Jesus' name, amen.

PART 3

HOPE, THE ANCHOR
OF OUR SOUL

The mountains are calling, and I must go.
JOHN MUIR

51 DROP ANCHOR ONCE MORE

We have this hope as an anchor for the soul, firm and secure.
HEBREWS 6:19

Friendships are important to me. I love making new friends and I hardly ever meet a stranger. Looking back over the years, one of the benefits of doing what I do for as long as I have is meeting so many different types of people all over the world. Consequently, I have made lots of wonderful friends, with many of my friendships lasting for decades. Of course, I have a circle of friends I'm closest to. They are the ones I trust and am most vulnerable with.

Perhaps that's why one of the hardest things I've had to overcome is the hurt I have felt when someone I trusted has betrayed me. It hasn't happened too many times, but one in particular wounded me deeply. I remember, as I was reeling from the shock of it all, I began to examine my heart, and I was surprised to realize that gradually, almost subconsciously, I had put my anchor—the one that was supposed to be reserved for Jesus and Jesus alone—in our friendship. I didn't mean to, but somewhere along the way I had put more emphasis on our friendship than perhaps I should have.

I had admired my friend, trusted her, confided in her, and when she hurt me it sent me spiraling into a place of angst and confusion and grief. I didn't know what had hit me. In that corner of my heart, without realizing it, I had pulled up anchor. Rather than being firmly anchored in Jesus, I realized that I was anchored in our friendship.

Have you ever discovered that your trust was in something other than Jesus? Maybe it happened when you went through a series of trials. In my experience, when the storms of life hit, and especially if they hit one right after the other, our anchoring in Jesus can become dislodged without us realizing it. To protect ourselves and survive, we can end up tethering ourselves to something else entirely. It can be people or positions, goals or career moves, money or prestige, even dreams or plans. It can literally be anything. Including a friendship.

It's such an easy thing to do—to drop our anchor in other places instead of in God and His Word—but when we do, we drift from having our hope firmly anchored in Jesus. And when we're not anchored, we can't endure. We'll drift with every current, letting it take us where we never wanted to go. Let's examine our hearts together today. Let's drop anchor in Jesus once more. Let's make sure we are firmly anchored in Him—and nothing else.

Heavenly Father, thank You for showing me if I have dropped anchor in anything or anyone else other than You. I put all my hopes in You, the true anchor of my soul. In Jesus' name, amen.

52 LET YOUR ANCHOR
DO HIS WORK

Now in this hope we were saved, but hope that is seen is not hope, because
who hopes for what he sees?
ROMANS 8:24

One time, when Nick and I were boating in one of our favorite little crystal-clear lagoons in Santorini, Greece—the same place we went on our honeymoon—he asked me to drop the anchor. No problem. Next, my plan was to close my eyes, take a nap, and relax in the sun. Nick's plan was to fish. Well, it wasn't too long into my well-planned nap that I awoke to a biting-cold wind, choppy waves, and murky waters.

To my shock, we had drifted all the way out into the shipping lanes where giant cargo ships cruise by. To top it off, a storm was brewing in the distance and headed right for us. Nick was already stowing his gear when he asked me if I had dropped the anchor.

"Yes, of course," I answered him.

"But did you set it?" he pressed further.

"Did I what? What are you talking about? You asked me to drop the anchor, and I did."

"Chris, if you don't ensure the anchor is attached to the ocean floor, then we aren't really anchored."

It's amazing the conversations you can get into with the people you love most at the worst possible moments, isn't it?

For hours, Nick fought the waves and the wind, and sometime long after dark, we pulled into a slip at the marina. We made it back safe and sound, but what I learned that day was far more than just the proper way to anchor a boat. I learned even more about Jesus, our Savior whom the writer of Hebrews described as this hope we have as an anchor for our souls.[24] It's only when we are firmly attached to our anchor—Jesus—that He can go to work and do His job. It's just as Paul described, "Hope that is seen is not hope, because who hopes for what he sees?"

Just like an anchor that is dug into the seabed far below the surface of the water, we can't see our hope at work. But our hope—Jesus—does His best work when we simply trust Him.

Think about this in light of your life right now. Are you feeling tossed about? Do you feel like you're drifting? Check your anchor. If we drop anchor and set it firmly in God, we might not know it's working at first, especially when everything is calm. But when the winds kick up, and the waves start to build, we will know it's doing what Jesus promised. If we keep our hope in Jesus, we can stay steady. Immovable. Firmly established. Ever enduring. Even in the strongest of currents and the worst of storms.

Heavenly Father, I drop anchor and set it in You once more. I trust You. I put my hope in You so I can stay steady, immovable, firmly established, ever enduring. In Jesus' name, amen.

53 LIVE AS A PRISONER

"Return to a stronghold, you prisoners who have hope; today I declare that I will restore double to you."

ZECHARIAH 9:12

F or seventy years the children of Israel were held in captivity in Babylon while the enemy pillaged their homeland. When they at last returned home, they found nothing but destruction. Even Jerusalem and the temple had to be rebuilt. But in the midst of their despair, Zechariah prophesied hope for their future.

God knew that the way for His people to escape their pit of despair—the same place of hopelessness in which we sometimes find ourselves—was for them to become "prisoners who have hope," or as other translations say, "prisoners of hope."[25] It was the way forward. The way to live enduring in their faith.

But how do any of us become such a thing? And what on earth does it even mean? Aren't prisoners people who are locked up in high-security institutions and stripped of all their freedoms? Why would we want to be characterized as a prisoner of anything, including hope?

Because a prisoner of hope in God is different. God's prisoners of hope aren't forced into an institution for punishment but are invited into a fortress for safety.

Imagine a castle that stands firm even when the very foundations of life are shaken. A place created just for us, where we can chain ourselves to the promise that God is working all things for our good, even when all things are falling apart.[26] From the high tower of this fortress, we prisoners of hope can see a whole new perspective. We can look beyond the circumstances surrounding us to the future, trusting that God has good things in store for us.

When I first learned to think and live this way, it was revolutionary to me. I was raised in a religious tradition that never encouraged me to expect good things from God. In fact, it was considered presumptuous to even imagine that God had time for my requests, given that He had an entire world to run. I'm so glad I discovered that despite the heartaches I have been through, He is still good and He wants to do good for me. He wants me to have hope, risk hope, get my hopes up, even after they are dashed once again. He wants this so much for me that He calls me to be a prisoner of hope.

Will you risk being one too? I know it can be unbelievably hard. There are unimaginable heartaches and excruciating losses that can come with life, and yet God extends a daring and loving invitation with an amazing promise: *Return . . . you prisoners of hope . . . I will restore double to you.*

Heavenly Father, with a deep breath I risk hope once more. In the face of loss and disappointment, even fear, I will risk hoping again. I will become a prisoner of hope. In Jesus' name, amen.

54 HOPE FOR OUR SHORTCOMINGS

I am sure of this, that he who started a good work in you will carry it on to completion until the day of Christ Jesus.
PHILIPPIANS 1:6

When I gave my heart fully to Jesus, everything in my life did not instantaneously change. I wish it had, but that's not how becoming a fully devoted follower of Christ works. It took years of submitting to God on my part and years of transforming me on God's part. I had rough edges that needed to be sanded smooth—in my words, attitudes, behaviors, in every area of my life. To this day, I'm still a work in progress. I'm still being transformed.

But when I was in my twenties and forging my way as a young leader, I began growing steadily, applying what I was learning about God and His Word. And though I made great strides, I still didn't always get it right. There were times I said and did things that inadvertently hurt others—my family, my coworkers, my friends. Nonetheless, I kept working at it all, doing my best to grow into a more mature Christ follower.

There were plenty of times I could have given up. I remember when I was leading one of my first teams and I was pushing them too hard. I overworked myself back then and just assumed everyone around me should do the same. A brave soul on my team came to me and put it all on the table. I remember being shocked. Hurt. Embarrassed. But once I took it all in, I was actually grateful. It wasn't something I couldn't change. It just stung to have to hear about it.

What I discovered in that experience is something I've come to cherish: God is a God of restoration and new beginnings. It's okay if we make mistakes. If we don't like where we are right now, we don't have to resign ourselves to it.

In God there is always hope—hope to change and to grow—because Jesus is always completing what He started in us. It is a process. When we are made aware of our shortcomings, we don't have to give up. We can repent, make right the things we can, and trust that God is still working in us and through us.

Have you blown it? Are you ready to grow again? Keep enduring by putting your hope in God. When we risk hoping, we open the door for change. We learn how to live in the present but with the future in mind. We shift the gaze of our focus forward. We become people of hope who are willing to let God surprise us with a new future. One where He completes what He has begun in us.

Heavenly Father, thank You for Your promise to finish what You have started in me. Help me grow and mature to the next level. Keep transforming me. In Jesus' name, amen.

55 HOP ANOTHER RIDE

Put your hope in the LORD. For there is faithful love with the LORD, and with him is redemption in abundance.

PSALM 130:7

When our girls were still young, we were so excited when someone gave us Australians a family trip to Disneyland. My girls were so excited to meet Mickey and Minnie, but secretly, I was most excited about all the rides. Sophia and I were hopping from one ride to another in Fantasyland when we boarded Peter Pan's Flight teeming with excitement to see Neverland. But as soon as we set sail, our fantasy came to an abrupt halt. The ride had broken, and the emergency lighting came on. Instead of seeing all that we were supposed to see—the Lost Boys battle Captain Hook, the fairies, and the infamous crocodile—we saw all that we were not supposed to see. I was utterly disappointed! My pixie-dust dreams had been shattered, so much so that Sophia looked at me and said, "It's okay, Mummy. These things happen. Can we go on the Alice in Wonderland ride now?"

I totally understand if you are laughing at me. Even writing this, it sounds ridiculous, but I really was disappointed. As I numbly got off the ride, all my expectations of hopeful adventure began to wane. And, quite literally, for the longest time, Disneyland didn't hold the magic it once had.

I know my story is silly, but what's not so silly is the life lesson I learned from Sophia. We both had the exact same experience but two totally different responses, and we ended up in two different places emotionally. I was stuck in a moment. She never was. I wasn't resilient, but Sophia was. She bounced right back.

I know the true disappointments in our lives are much bigger and far more sobering. I don't have all the answers for why gut-wrenching heartache happens to us. Still, I know from my own experiences that if we are going to fulfill our purposes in this earth and stay hopeful and on mission, we must accept that some things will break down along the way.

The ride may come to a surprising stop.

Dim emergency lighting may be all we have to light our way through a dark season.

But we can't let it cause us to be stuck in a moment in time. To keep enduring, to keep moving forward, we will have to learn how to manage our disappointments well, so we can hop on another ride full of renewed hope. Otherwise, we'll miss all the adventure God has set before us.

Do you feel stuck in a moment? Do you want to get unstuck? Risk putting your hopes and dreams and trust in God once more. When you do, He promises faithful love and redemption in abundance.

Heavenly Father, I want to move forward. I want to get unstuck, so I put my hope in You once more. I trust You. In Jesus' name, amen.

56 KEEP YOUR
FAITH ALIVE

If a brother or sister is without clothes and lacks daily food and one of you says to them, "Go in peace, stay warm, and be well fed," but you don't give them what the body needs, what good is it? In the same way faith, if it does not have works, is dead by itself.

JAMES 2:15–17

'll never forget the time when Sophia was little and she got away from me on a busy street. I was holding her hand as we raced from place to place running errands when all of a sudden, I realized her hand was no longer in mine. If you've ever had one of your kids beside you only to look down and see them gone, then you know the level of anxiety that gripped my heart.

When I frantically looked down and back through the crowd, desperate for a glimpse of her sweet face, I spotted her crouched down in front of a homeless man. She was handing him a dollar bill I had given her that morning. She had been so indecisive at every stop we'd made, debating on how to spend it. On a trinket? A piece of candy? A toy? And there she was, just handing it over to this man.

By the time I reached her side, I heard her saying, "Jesus gave me this dollar to give to you."

Then I watched as the man gave it back, and with tears streaming down his face, he said, "Honey, you spend it on some candy for yourself."

I was overcome with so many emotions all at once. I was beyond relieved to find her and overwhelmed at the goodness of God in her. I was grateful she wasn't numb to someone who was asking for help. I have always wanted my girls' eyes to be open, to really see people, and to be moved to act with compassion. And I've wanted them to understand that our faith is expressed through our works. It's an incredible feeling when we realize our children have grasped something so important.

We are Jesus' hands and feet to our world. There is something that happens in our hearts when we put action to our faith, whether that's just taking the next step we feel God nudging us to take or when we step into the lives of the vulnerable and lend a helping hand.

Let's be as generous as Sophia was that day. Let's see what and who others might be overlooking. Let's make it a point to put action to our faith. To help someone. To touch someone. To encourage someone. To keep our faith alive.

Father, show me who I can touch today to make their world brighter. Show me how I can keep my faith alive doing the works You've called me to do. In Jesus' name, amen.

57 HE IS WITH US!

"The LORD is the one who will go before you. He will be with you; he will not leave you or abandon you. Do not be afraid or discouraged." Moses wrote down this law and gave it to the priests, the sons of Levi, who carried the ark of the LORD's covenant, and to all the elders of Israel.

DEUTERONOMY 31:8–9

For forty years the children of Israel wandered in the wilderness. When I took my girls on a road trip to Joshua Tree National Park in California, I couldn't help but think of the Israelites, because more than two-thirds of Joshua Tree National Park is described as wilderness. Upward of half a million acres lie in the overlap between the Colorado and Mojave deserts, and it's filled with Joshua trees and scrub. As I made sure we read every informative sign and thoroughly investigated the visitor center—yes, I'm that mother—I kept trying to imagine what it would be like to spend almost half my lifetime in such arid conditions, winding my way around the cacti and pitching my tent in the sand. I love the great outdoors, but I'm not sure I would have been a happy camper if I had spent forty years of my life walking from one campsite to the next.

It's comforting to know that the children of Israel were never alone in their desert adventures. From today's verse we know that as Moses was about to turn his leadership over to Joshua, the ark of the covenant was still with them. It was the place of God's presence. The priests had carried it every step of the way from the time it was built, right after God gave Moses the Ten Commandments. It was with them all the way to the moment when Joshua was getting ready to lead them across the Jordan River into the promised land. The ark of the covenant was God's way of being with His people.

Once Jesus came, He made a way for God's Spirit to live inside of us, so the ark was no longer the place of His presence. This means that just as the children of Israel never had to be alone, we don't ever have to either. If we have invited Jesus into our hearts; if we have given our lives to Him fully, His Holy Spirit lives in us and is with us at all times. How comforting to know that any wilderness we walk through, He is with us!

If fear or discouragement is displacing your faith, remember that He's right there with you. Just like He promised the children of Israel, He will never leave you or abandon you. Keep enduring and watch Him take you all the way through your wilderness and into your promised land.

Heavenly Father, thank You that You are with me and will never abandon me. I find my courage in You and in Your presence. In Jesus' name, amen.

58 RECOGNIZE JESUS

That same day two of them were on their way to a village called Emmaus. . . . Together they were discussing everything that had taken place. And while they were discussing and arguing, Jesus himself came near and began to walk along with them. But they were prevented from recognizing him.

LUKE 24:13–16

The disciples who faithfully followed Jesus looked forward to a future full of hope. But when He was crucified, when events did not unfold as they'd anticipated, their world came apart. Two of them lost all hope and headed home to Emmaus. Even with all that was being said in Jerusalem, they did not believe Jesus was alive. Not even when He came alongside them and began walking with them. Lost in their disappointment, they did not recognize Him.

Have you ever been in such a place? Where you were so disillusioned—so lost in your concerns—that even if God had walked alongside you and begun to talk, you quite possibly wouldn't have heard Him? I feel sure I have.

If we were to follow all the steps of these two disciples on the road to Emmaus, we'd find that their journey through disappointment and disillusionment to renewed hope is often the same path we follow. When Jesus first began talking to them, they were so discouraged they couldn't pick up on His voice.[27] It's only when I've worked through my disappointment and gotten a more heavenly perspective that my hearing has been restored—and my hope.

As they kept walking, still utterly crushed, the Bible says they wouldn't even look up, so they couldn't see Him walking alongside them. As long as we look down at our circumstances, and not up at Him, we'll miss what He wants us to see.

As they kept going, they asked Jesus if He had any idea of the disappointing events that had taken place.[28] When Jesus answered, He brought them back to the Word.[29] Jesus knew the promises of God and explained how those promises would be fulfilled in a way that would change the world. He told them that a new kingdom was at hand. Jesus knew what we need to remember: it is the Word that changes our perspective from disappointment to hope.

Finally, at the end of their journey, the disciples invited Jesus to join them for a meal. It was only when Jesus broke the bread that their eyes were opened. They recognized Him in the midst of their disappointment, and their hope was renewed.[30]

I want to remind you today that in the midst of your disappointment, Jesus is there with you. He has not left you. He has not forgotten you. Dare to look up, and as you see Him, your hope will be renewed.

Father, You are the God of all hope. I listen for You. I look up to see You. Thank You for renewing my hope and building endurance in me. In Jesus' name, amen.

59 ACKNOWLEDGE
HIS PRESENCE

"What things?" [Jesus] asked them. So [the two disciples] said to him, "The things concerning Jesus of Nazareth, who was a prophet powerful in action and speech before God and all the people, and how our chief priests and leaders handed him over to be sentenced to death, and they crucified him. But we were hoping that he was the one who was about to redeem Israel. Besides all this, it's the third day since these things happened."

LUKE 24:19–21

After the resurrection, when Jesus was walking with the two disciples who were on their way back to their hometown of Emmaus, they did not realize it was Jesus who was walking with them. As the disciples were discussing everything that had taken place, even arguing about it, Jesus asked them what they were talking about. I find this hilarious. Jesus had to know what they were discussing because He's God. Still, He asked.

One of the disciples, Cleopas, answered Him with a question of his own; I'll paraphrase it for you: "Seriously? Where have you been? You must be the only person who doesn't know the things that have been happening."

The dialogue just kept getting better, and Jesus asked the next question: "What things?"

As the disciples went on to answer Him, still not recognizing that He was Jesus, the One they were so downcast and heartbroken over, they said, "But we were hoping . . ." Another translation says, "We had hoped . . ."[31]

What a telling phrase. Is there something that turned out a different way than you had hoped? Was there something you had hoped about a relationship? Was there something you had hoped about a business deal? Was there something you had hoped about a medical report? Was there something you had hoped about a new opportunity?

How the disciples felt is as relevant today as it was back then. How many times have we had high hopes and expectations about something, only to have it all not work out? We've all had our own versions of a "we had hoped" journey, haven't we?

Take your "I had hoped" to Jesus today. A key to getting through any disappointment in life—to enduring in our faith—is being able to acknowledge the presence of God with us in the midst of our disappointment, in our hurt, in our betrayal, in our disillusionment. Right there in that place.

Whether you realize it or not, He's walking right alongside you wherever you are—be it in a dark place or a joyous one. Be it on a treacherous path or a smooth one. Be it moving uphill or downhill. He's right there with you. The omnipresence of God assures us that wherever we are, God is there. Take a moment and acknowledge Him today. Acknowledge His presence and dare to hope again.

Jesus, help me to see You, hear You, and feel Your presence with me. Thank You for being with me in every minute of my life. In Your name I pray, amen.

60 OVERFLOW WITH HOPE

May the God of hope fill you with all joy and peace as you believe so that you may overflow with hope by the power of the Holy Spirit.
ROMANS 15:13

When I was still in my early twenties, I enrolled at a local Bible college, mostly because everything about following Jesus was so new to me. Part of the coursework required that I speak in chapel, which was like a mini church service where the students took turns speaking short messages from Scripture.

When it was my turn, I felt so much trepidation that to this day I can't even remember what I said. But I do remember what someone said to me afterward: that it was obvious that I was not gifted to speak, and it was highly unlikely anyone would ever invite me to speak.

As you can imagine, I was absolutely devastated. If I'd had any hope up to that point of influencing even one person on the earth, all my hopes were dashed. One person's words crushed whatever ounce of courage I had mustered that day. I can't even begin to describe how many months of confidence those words took from my life. The energy, the effort, to find the willingness to work through it internally took even longer.

Have anyone's words ever done something like that to you? I imagine the Enemy has made sure we've all taken such a hit. Especially in an area targeted to our calling.

Once I picked myself up, emotionally and spiritually, I risked looking to Jesus and hoping once again. As I did—as I endured—I began learning something that forever affected the trajectory of my life. God wanted me to learn resilience. He wanted me to place my hope in Him. Not in my abilities. Not in people's opinions of me. Not in their accolades or their criticism. It was just the first installment in such lessons, but by far one of the most significant, and it's grown into a lifelong process of development. I could have quit that day and never become the Jesus follower I have grown to be. I could have walked away from all the purpose God had in mind. I had every reason to give in to hopelessness and abandon the future God had planned for me. But I didn't. Instead, I began declaring that my hope is in God and God alone. And I've never quit.

Don't you quit either. No matter what someone has said. No matter how dashed your hopes have been. I understand that when we get blindsided by something, it's so easy to grow afraid to hope again, but God wants us turn to Him to fill us with all joy and peace as we believe, so that we may overflow with hope by the power of the Holy Spirit.

Heavenly Father, my hope is in You and You alone. Thank You that I overflow with hope by the power of the Holy Spirit. In Jesus' name, amen.

61 GOD IS OUR HOPE

Not only that, but we also boast in our afflictions, because we know that affliction produces endurance, endurance produces proven character, and proven character produces hope.

ROMANS 5:3–4

From the time Sophia was a toddler and started talking, she has been a quirky, happy, and fun-loving girl. She loves theater and acts out everything from Broadway to historical speeches. Boldly. Loudly. Joyfully. For the whole world to hear. So when she was in middle school and started being unusually quiet for a couple of weeks, my motherly antennae went up.

Though I asked a couple of times if everything was all right, she deflected each time and insisted nothing was wrong. So I waited. Patiently. Watchfully. Until one night when it all came spilling out. Friends at school had begun to make fun of her, exclude her, and talk about her. She was bewildered, shocked, and heartbroken. Listening to her recount it all, I couldn't help but cry on the inside as tears streamed down her face.

If you've ever navigated a child through middle school drama, you know how gut-wrenching such things can be. For that matter, we all remember middle school, don't we? Even if it went relatively well for you, it's such a season of change and awkward growth.

As I helped her move through that season and manage her disappointment, I wanted so badly to tell her that once middle school was over, all her relational challenges would end and she would live happily ever after. But that isn't true for any of us. Instead, I told her in an age-appropriate way what I'd say to all of us.

This journey of following Jesus means that if we are going to keep our hearts open, soft, sensitive, and connected to humanity, we must realize that we are never going to be bulletproof to unexpected pain and heartache. No matter how carefully we pick our friends or our spouses. No matter how carefully we manage our finances. No matter how well we vet the company or ministry we work for. Life will happen.

What will make the difference is how we manage our disappointment. Do we let all the middle school drama that happens throughout life stop us from ever trusting again? Ever risking relationships again? Ever hoping again? However you've been hurt, tell God all about it. He can handle it, even if you feel He's the One who let you down. Yes, I just said that. He knows how we feel, so it's better just to say it. Then, let's invite Him in. Let's invite His healing presence to come so we can hope once more. After all, affliction produces endurance. Endurance produces proven character. Proven character, hope. In the face of anything, God is our hope.

Heavenly Father, I boast in my afflictions, because I know that my afflictions produce endurance, and my endurance produces proven character, and my proven character produces hope. In You, I am hopeful and hope-filled. In Jesus' name, amen.

62 LOOK PAST THE RUINS

LORD, *you showed favor to your land; you restored the fortunes of Jacob. You forgave your people's guilt; you covered all their sin. Selah You withdrew all your fury; you turned from your burning anger.*

PSALM 85:1–3

When the children of Israel made it back home, after spending seventy years as captives in Babylon, they came home to rubble. They came back to find the temple destroyed, the city in ruins, and enemies surrounding them on every side. Instead of finding everything the way they had left it and remembered it, they found nothing but destruction. They were expecting to pick back up where they left off with their pre-exilic life. They were expecting to get back to normal, but normal was completely gone.

What a familiar place. No doubt we've all been there when we just wanted everything to get back to normal, but sometimes that doesn't happen. As much as the children of Israel hoped and expected post-captivity life to be one way, it was an entirely different way. What ensued then was discouragement, disillusionment, and disappointment. A sense of hopelessness. They even lost their faith.

It's so easy to do when circumstances, seasons, and expectations wind up being different from the way we had hoped. For me, there have been initiatives I've launched where I thought everything would go one way, but it went an entirely different way. There have been events I've planned where I imagined every detail, and nothing went according to plan. There have been projects I've mapped out that took a turn and finished up looking entirely different from what I expected. There have been relationships that I just knew would flourish, but they turned out to do quite the opposite.

What do we do when something we looked forward to and had high hopes for doesn't unfold quite like we had hoped? Maybe we should look back at what the children of Israel did when they found their homeland in ruins: They composed a song—Psalm 85—and then they used it in their prayer services. They incorporated it into their liturgy. And it became a way of basically declaring, "Let's have a revival!" To kick it off, they recounted God's faithfulness to them. They directed their worship to Him. Look at what they said to God: "You showed Your favor. You restored. You forgave. You covered. You withdrew. You turned."

What a beautiful way to look past all the ruins. To rekindle hope! To kickstart faith! To endure what has turned out differently than anyone expected. What an example for us to follow. Dare to look past the ruins in your life today. Declare your faith and hope in the One who has been faithful before. Recount your blessings, and kick off a revival in your heart!

Heavenly Father, I look past everything that didn't turn out the way I expected, and I put my hope in You once more. Thank You for all You've done for me! In Jesus' name, amen.

63 HOPE AGAINST HOPE

He [Abraham] believed, hoping against hope, so that he became the father of many nations according to what had been spoken: So will your descendants be.

ROMANS 4:18

When God gave Abraham such an outlandish and unexpected promise—that he would be the father of many nations—he believed God's promise. He risked hope against all rational hope. He didn't deny the facts of his circumstances—that he and Sarah were too old to have any children at all—but he refused to believe his circumstances were the whole truth, because they did not account for God's promise. He did not waver or doubt, and because of that, his faith grew even stronger. When, at last, Isaac was born—roughly twenty-five years later—Abraham gave all the glory to God.

Imagine the difference we could make if we learned to face the unexpected in our lives the way Abraham did. If we learned to do the unexpected while facing the unexpected. What if we believed instead of feared in the face of the unknown? What if we courageously moved through loss and disappointment, believing God has purpose for it on the other side? What if we got up every day believing God for the best, knowing we might possibly encounter the worst? What if we dared get our hopes up when there was no foreseeable reason to have any hope at all? Isn't that what Abraham did? He hoped against all hope. He believed when all indicators appeared to be hopeless.

I don't say this lightly. I fully understand how circumstantially and physically some things really can be defined as impossible. As utterly hopeless. Because they are. But in the face of such things, we still can have hope in God—in His nature, in His character, in His devotion to us. Even when the circumstances have no natural hope of changing.

Hope in God is the perfect solution when we're facing the impossible. When we have more questions than answers. More doubt than faith. Hope is unshakable confidence in God Himself. It doesn't deny the reality of our pain, but it does give us a life beyond our pain. It gives us permission to believe in a new beginning and to keep enduring. It is the happy and confident expectation of good that lifts our spirits and dares us to believe for a different future. It is always looking to God with expectation.

I believe we can live this expectantly—this hopefully, this freely, this faith-filled—in the face of *everything* that comes our way.

What are you facing today that has been labeled hopeless? Dare to put your hope in God, in who He is. Dare to look above your circumstances to Him. Dare to hope against all hope.

Heavenly Father, I put my hope in You. I look above the impossible and the hopeless in my life, and hope anyway . . . in You, the God of all hope. I hope against all hope. In Jesus' name, amen.

64 KEEP MOVING THROUGH

When you pass through the waters, I will be with you, and the rivers will not overwhelm you. When you walk through the fire, you will not be scorched, and the flame will not burn you.

ISAIAH 43:2

When I was diagnosed with cancer in my thyroid gland a number of years ago, I was bombarded with so many emotions and the need to make serious decisions. Should I have surgery or not? Would I need any subsequent treatments? If you've been through such a diagnosis or walked through it with a friend or loved one, you are familiar with how it can be a lot to take in.

I knew the devastating effects of cancer in a deeply personal way. I had seen my dad fade away from me when I was just nineteen. It left a mark on us all—Mum, my brothers, and me. We lost our hero at a crucial time in our lives and we were never the same. So, naturally, when I heard my diagnosis, instead of facing it and going through whatever might be on the road ahead, I wanted to be delivered *from* it all.

Time and time again, I had learned to run *to* God and not *from* Him. I had learned that whatever my situation, He was there with me. I had taken it to heart that God is good, and I believed in His goodness. So I put my hope in Him once more. It would have been great to know *why* I had to go through it all, but sometimes we don't even get to know that—and the deliverance we often hope for comes by walking through what's before us, one step at a time.

It's tempting to think that because a season is painful and difficult, God isn't there. But that's not what He promised. He said, "When you pass through the waters, I will be with you. . . . When you walk through the fire, you will not be scorched." What's more, each and every time we walk through the fire, He is building endurance in us. How many times have you gone through something only to come out the other side stronger? I feel sure I have every single time. And walking through the surgery I eventually had was no different.

Are you going through something today that you had hoped you'd be delivered from? Keep moving through, knowing He is with you. Keep moving through, trusting that He's doing something in you. Keep moving through, continuing to live a life of purpose and passion, never losing sight of what God has created you and called you to do.

Heavenly Father, I put my trust in You for what I'm moving through. Thank You for Your plans for me, for my well-being, to give me a future and a hope. In Your name I pray, amen.

65 EPIC HOPE

Hope delayed makes the heart sick, but desire fulfilled is a tree of life.
PROVERBS 13:12

C anceled again! Can you believe it? That's three years in a row I'm not getting to race!" Nick exclaimed.

For three years Nick had been training in hopes of riding in the Cape Epic in South Africa—one of the world's most athletically challenging mountain bike races. It's an eight-day race across more than four hundred miles of untamed terrain, with a total vertical ascent of more than fifty thousand feet, depending on the route, which changes every year.[32]

The first year, Nick trained for a year in advance, which meant anywhere from three to six hours of riding at a time. Then he traveled all the way to South Africa and started the race, but three days in, he grew really, really sick. The officials wouldn't let him finish the race because he nearly had kidney failure. He still raised a fantastic sum for the work of A21, which was his goal all along, but he was so disappointed about having to drop out of the race.

The next year, after another year of intense training, he flew to Cape Town, only to have the pandemic of 2020 begin and countries start shutting their borders and canceling such events. It was pretty touch and go as he went from country to country trying to get home before they closed the airports. I was never so glad to have him home.

When Nick learned that the race of 2021 was canceled as well, it was hard not to feel heartsick. After all, once again, he'd been training for two years. Have you ever worked hard only to have everything you planned for, worked for, trained for, saved for, come to nothing? Hope delayed does make the heart sick, doesn't it?

I've reminded Nick more than once that maybe all this training is to ride in the Cape Epic of heaven and not South Africa! I'm not being insensitive to all he's invested in this dream, but I'm reminding him that our hope ultimately is in Jesus. Not in all the things we plan and look forward to here on earth. Some of our longings will be fulfilled only on the other side of the veil. If we keep our hope in Jesus and all that He is, when things don't go the way we thought they would, we won't be as disappointed. We'll be able to endure full of hope! Sure, we'll have to deal with it, but it won't consume our thoughts and moods for days on end. We'll look up quickly and thank Jesus He has something better in mind. Let's have epic hope today—hope that's in Jesus and Jesus alone.

Jesus, my hope is in You and You alone. I trust You no matter how my circumstances evolve here on earth. You are my epic hope! In Your name I pray, amen.

66 OUR ACTUAL
SOURCE OF HOPE

The one who has the Son has life. The one who does not have the Son of God does not have life.

1 JOHN 5:12

Of all the churches I've had the privilege of attending around the globe, the church in Qatar was unlike any other. I was there on a Friday, their designated church day, and we had to go way beyond the city limits of Doha to reach a religious compound where the government had given all the Christian denominations space to build their churches.

To get to the building where I was to speak, we had to pass through three checkpoints that were heavily guarded. At each one, we had to show our passports and confirm that we were Christians, as it would have been unlawful for any Muslims to enter the compound.

As much as any of the churchgoers might want others to know they were Christian, perhaps with something as simple as a cross or scripture displayed on their desks at work, they were never allowed to even hint at their faith outside their weekly services inside the compound.

Most of the people attending the different churches had to park outside the compound and walk all the way to their buildings. I marveled that despite the heat, the distance, the risk, the difficulty, the danger, the checkpoints, and the limits on when and how and where they could acknowledge their devotion to Christ, they came. They endured. As the people poured into their respective churches, it was obvious they were full of joy and enthusiasm. They could not wait to worship King Jesus. I was both inspired and challenged by their deep sense of hope. I realized their hope was in Christ alone, and that is what brought them joy. Their hope was not in any of the things I take for granted. They did not have the same freedoms that I did, and yet their hope seemed more anchored than mine.

Have you ever come across a situation that made you realize how much you really have, all because of what you see others don't have, and it caused you to reexamine where you put your hope? Qatar was that for me. I have always lived where I can go to church when I want wherever I want. I've never had to hide that I am a follower of Jesus, and yet there have been many times when I have lost hope because I put my hope in things and people other than Jesus. There have been times when I have forgotten who was my actual source of hope.

What about you? What has caught your attention like this? Think about that today and be sure all your hope is in Jesus and Jesus alone.

Jesus, search my heart and show me where I've put my hope in anything or anyone other than You. You are the One who gives me life. In Your name I pray, amen.

67 THE HOPE WITHIN

Do not fear them or be intimidated, but in your hearts regard Christ the Lord as holy, ready at any time to give a defense to anyone who asks you for a reason for the hope that is in you.
1 PETER 3:14–15

I like to join new gyms from time to time, partly to keep myself inspired to work out, and partly to meet new people who might not have discovered Jesus yet. I always enjoy meeting new people, and if I get to share Jesus with them, all the better.

At one gym, I quickly became friends with a woman I often crossed paths with on the treadmill. She was in her late forties, single, and focused on her career. For weeks we ran alongside one another, reminding each other we could make it to the end of another workout. Over time, we shared stories, including some about our personal lives. I learned that she was recently divorced after finding her husband in an affair.

In turn, she learned that Nick and I had been married for more than two decades. One day she asked me why, after being married so long, I wouldn't want to "get out there" and find more variety.

I knew how I answered her question would make all the difference in her ever asking me anything again. I wanted to speak in such a way that I met her need to be loved, accepted, and valued. I wanted it to be an opportunity to share with her the reason for the hope that is within me.

I thoughtfully shared my biblical views and my faith in Jesus in a nonjudgmental way. I explained how I based my decisions on the Bible, and that as a follower of Jesus, I believe marriage is a covenant between a man and a woman. I shared my heart that I never want to do anything to jeopardize the love and trust Nick and I share. And then, to keep it from being too heavy, I joked, "Why would I want to have anyone else when I have the best?"

She was blown away by my perspective. So many men she met online were married and had no issue with having affairs. She was astounded that Nick and I wouldn't consider it. I was relieved that answering her honestly about the hope I have in Jesus, which serves as the foundation of my marriage, prompted a dozen more questions. It didn't shut them down.

When was the last time you got to share about the hope that is within you and how that hope—Jesus—directs every facet of your life? How that hope helps you endure? Look for opportunities today, and share with tenderness. Remember: we have to be winsome if we want to win some.

Jesus, thank You for opportunities to share about the hope that is within me. To tell others of who You are and what You've done in my life. In Your name I pray, amen.

68 OUR OVERARCHING HOPE

Now if we hope for what we do not see, we eagerly wait for it with patience.
ROMANS 8:25

When my elder daughter, Catherine, was in high school, she tried out for the volleyball team every year. Each year she made it, we were all relieved, because in the weeks leading up to the tryouts, inside our home, we could all feel her anxiety. There were times when the pressure felt so intense, Nick and Sophia and I all thought we were trying out for the team too!

When she graduated and it came time to apply for college, it felt like volleyball tryouts all over again. I had to work at not feeling anxious that she wouldn't be accepted at the schools where she most wanted to go. As we waited to hear from each school, it wasn't easy on my heart hearing her say over and over, "Oh Mum, I hope I get in."

When we hope and hope for something, and it doesn't happen, we can be so disappointed. It's not wrong to hope for what we want, but it's so much better to hope in Jesus—and not just for what we want. When we don't get what we want, when we want, the way we want, it's such a setup for disappointment. Of course, not hoping isn't the answer either. Feelings of hopelessness can leave us wanting to pull back and rewrite the rest of our lives as a smaller, safer story than the adventurous one God originally planned for us. It's so easy to grow afraid to hope again.

No matter what we've faced, Jesus wants us to find a way to hope again. He wants us to hope in His Word. He wants us to hope in His promises—for joy, for peace, for love. For the fruit of the Spirit. For His nature and His character. For the security that can be found only in Him. He wants us to hope with His hope that resonates on the inside of us and isn't solely dependent on what happens around us—or to us.

When Catherine finally did get in to one of her top picks, we all rejoiced! It was such a relief. But it was the perfect season to remind her where our trust truly lies and how we can endure fulfilling all God's plans and purposes for our lives. What if she hadn't gotten into any of the schools? She's brilliant, but I knew from other parents it was a possibility. All the more reason I had to put my hope in Jesus too.

What are you hoping for? Keep watching and waiting for it, but make sure the overarching hope in your heart is grounded more in Jesus than anything else.

Jesus, my greatest hope is in You. Whatever happens, I put all my hopes in You, and I trust that Your plans and purposes for my life will prevail, regardless of what happens. In Your name, amen.

69 SHARING HOPE

I am certain that I will see the LORD's goodness in the land of the living.
PSALM 27:13

When the pandemic of 2020 landed us all at home more than we ever expected to be, Nick and I got to know our neighbors in ways we never had the opportunity to before. One day as I set the trash out at the end of our drive, I met up with our next-door neighbor, who was doing the same. When I casually remarked, "Good morning! It's a great day!" in an instant, I could tell by the look on his face he did not feel quite the same sentiment. "What? How can you say that?" he said, "The world's falling apart."

I was well aware of the tragic time in which we were living. I had friends who had or were suffering with COVID-19. We had staff fighting through it. I knew people who had died. I had wept. I had grieved. I had stood in faith and processed negative news day after day and week after week. All the more reason to put my hope in the Lord.

One translation of today's verse says, "I would have despaired had I not believed that I would see the goodness of the LORD."[33] Never was that truer than during the pandemic.

What my neighbor didn't know and didn't understand is that I was talking hope. Though I didn't know how things were going to turn out for him and his job and family, for me and my family and my life of traveling and speaking, I did know that God was in control. He didn't cause the pandemic, but He was in the midst of it with us.

As Nick and I began to do more than say, "Hi," in passing, we got to know our neighbors better. In time, we agreed to have weekly on-the-lawn, socially distanced get-togethers. Each week we talked about everything. Our work with A21. Their careers. Our girls. Their grown children. The economy. And how this was all going to affect our futures. The best part was that Nick and I got to explain this hope that we have—this confidence we live with, believing God above all else. This certainty we move forward with even when everything around is completely uncertain. This reason we have for enduring.

Have you ever gotten to share where your hope comes from? I'll always be grateful for the good that came out of such a tragic time. Our neighbors moved away, but they took a new understanding with them. An understanding that comes only from God and has the power to carry us through even the most unexpected time in our generation. Hope.

Father, I too would have despaired had I not believed that I would see the goodness of the Lord in the land of the living. My enduring faith and hope are in You. In Jesus' name, amen.

70 NEED A RETHINK?

For then you will have a future, and your hope will not be dashed.
PROVERBS 23:18

When COVID-19 first began spreading in early 2020 and mandatory stay-at-home orders were issued in cities and states across the US and countries around the globe, my entire speaking schedule was suddenly up in the air. Life as we all knew it was completely upended. Overnight it seemed our girls began learning how to do school from home, Nick was officing in the garage, and I was finishing up a book on the kitchen counter. We all have our story, don't we?

I remember one day, as I was trying to wrap my heart and mind around what was happening, I wrestled my faith and frustrations at the same time. Nick was listening to me work through it all when I recounted the additional Propel events we'd planned and what great hopes we had for what the Lord was going to do in those meetings. We had prayerfully planned them, so how could we be canceling them? At one point, without really thinking, I said, "I was hoping this year we would break through on so many levels, and it's like all hope is lost." Yes, I really said that.

Nick was so kind, and he understood my disappointment, but he knew I couldn't stay there. He knew I wouldn't want to stay there; so, knowing me like he does, he helped me get my head back in the right space. "What do you mean?" he ventured. "Jesus is still on the throne.

He hasn't gone anywhere. If our hope is in Jesus and Jesus alone, how could all hope be lost?"

It was the rethink I needed. I'm so glad that when I'm disappointed or I start to panic over something, Nick holds steady. I'm so glad when I start to lose hope, he doesn't. We all need someone in our lives like that—a spouse, a friend, a mentor. He balances me out and puts me in remembrance of what we both believe. Jesus is on the throne, and there's always reason to hope in Him—even when our best-made plans have to be canceled. The key is not to misplace our hope and put it in whatever plans or goals we had made. That's what sets us up for disappointment. That's what sabotages our endurance. But when we put our hope in Jesus, we put it in the eternal hope that can trump our temporal disappointments every single time.

Where have you put your hope? Do you need a rethink? If it's in Jesus, then it's impossible for all hope to be lost. He's still on the throne. He's still at work. He's still watching over us all.

Jesus, I realign my hope and move it from being in my goals and dreams and plans and put it all in You, because You are hope. In Your name I pray, amen.

71 WHOLEHEARTED HOPE

"But since my servant Caleb has a different spirit and has remained loyal to me, I will bring him into the land where he has gone, and his descendants will inherit it."

NUMBERS 14:24

Out of the million or so men Moses led out of Egypt and across the desert on an eleven-day journey that evolved into a forty-year quest, Caleb was one of only two men who actually stepped foot across the Jordan River into the promised land.[34] The other was Joshua. A generation died in the wilderness, and two other generations were born. Hanging on to the promises of God, Joshua and Caleb lived through it all and saw the land flowing with milk and honey.[35] They never forgot all that God had done for them; they endured and remained faith-filled and hope-filled for decades.

Caleb, in particular, had a different spirit, the Bible says. When, at forty years of age, Moses sent him to spy out the land, he came back with a wholehearted report. He told Moses they should go and take possession of the land, that they could certainly do it.[36] He was positive. The other scouts, however, were negative and fearful. All they could see were the giants; they said they felt as small as grasshoppers in comparison.[37] But not Caleb, and because of that God promised him that he would get to go into Canaan and that his descendants would inherit it.[38]

God rewarded Caleb, and Caleb never let go of what God promised. Forty-five years later, at age eighty-five, he was just as wholehearted. Just as hopeful. He wasn't quitting until he got what he'd fought more than forty years to get. He wasn't quitting until he got to move to Hebron in the promised land.

From the beginning, Caleb wasn't the most gifted, or most eloquent, or the smartest. But he was the most wholehearted and he remained loyal. There's nothing more inspiring than someone who stays hopeful for a specific promise over the course of forty years, which is exactly what he did. He endured until he saw the promise.

What is the longest you've ever hoped for something before it came to pass? Perhaps you're still waiting, still standing, still hoping. Maybe it's for a loved one to be saved. To be healed. To be free. What has God promised you? Hold on to your promise the way Caleb did—wholeheartedly, full of faith and full of hope.

Heavenly Father, thank You for Your promises to me, recorded in Your Word. I put my hope and trust in You. I will stay hopeful for as long as it takes. In Jesus' name, amen.

72 WHERE'S YOUR HOPE?

Why, my soul, are you so dejected? Why are you in such turmoil? Put your hope in God, for I will still praise him, my Savior and my God.
PSALM 42:11

The day that my mum unexpectedly passed away, my brother had helped her FaceTime with me. It was my fiftieth birthday and she wanted to wish me happy birthday. She had been declining in health, but in recent weeks she seemed to have stabilized. Knowing I was flying home to see her in two weeks did both our hearts good. When I spoke with my brother later that night and listened to how she'd slipped peacefully away, I was in shock. I knew she wouldn't last forever, but I thought we would have more time. To this day, what I cherish most is that last call, seeing her smiling face, telling her, "I love you, Mum," and hearing her say, "I love you too."

In the following days, as I prepared to fly home, I couldn't help but be sad. I was so heartbroken. I loved her dearly. It made no sense.

Have you ever been through such a shock, through something that took you completely by surprise, when you had been hoping for something else entirely? What do we do when we hope for something so deeply, that means so much, and it doesn't happen at all the way we've imagined? Worse yet, it turns out in a way that brings such terrible heartache and sadness. Such grief and disappointment. Do we lose all hope?

Do we start asking questions, maybe even start doubting what we once believed? How deeply do unexpected shocks rattle us? In such circumstances, it's easy to go so far as to think that it's God who has let us down. Have you ever felt that way?

I understand how hard it can be to face such an idea, but telling God how we honestly feel is a good step forward for us, and it's a good step toward Him. As I got through my initial shock and grief, my hope was in Christ. Because of that, I could keep enduring strong in faith. By the time we flew to Australia for Mum's funeral, I was in a place to receive the grace I needed to be a strength to my brothers and their families.

If a shock has caused your hope to shift from being firmly anchored in Jesus, reset it in Him today. Tell Him how you honestly feel and risk putting your hope in Jesus once more.

Heavenly Father, I put my hope in You. I look up and over my circumstances. Come what may, I will not be moved because I put my hope in You. You are my anchor. Not what happens here on earth. In Jesus' name, amen.

73 RECENTER YOUR HOPE

God wanted to make known among the Gentiles the glorious wealth of this mystery, which is Christ in you, the hope of glory.
COLOSSIANS 1:27

When Sophia graduated middle school, it was during the strangest of times. Everyone was doing their best trying not to catch COVID-19, so to keep everyone safe, her school hosted an outdoor celebration in the parking lot. Nick and I, and all the other families, sat in our cars and watched as our children were all spaced six feet apart, waiting to walk across the stage. The staff did a great job making the best of the situation, but you couldn't escape the surreal feeling that hung in the air. We all knew this wasn't normal. That tragic things were happening. But we were a united front, honking and clapping, to give our kids the love, encouragement, and stability we were all trying to hold on to.

If your child's graduation was held outside, I'm sure it's an unforgettable memory for you too. There were so many alternatives, including drive-through graduations and online events. The creativity people showed around the world was impressive.

And yet underneath it all remained a world of disappointments. Weddings were canceled. Long-planned vacations were canceled. Trips to see loved ones in health-care facilities couldn't happen. Jobs were lost. For so many of us, it was unfathomable to have friends let us know they were in the hospital, only to learn later they were on a ventilator or that they didn't recover.

Being able to navigate disappointment, especially in a season when we naturally feel overrun, is no small thing. And life during the pandemic had to be the hardest of all. But even then, in the face of what was undeniably overwhelming, Jesus was still our only hope.

There were days I was reminded I had no more control over situations than anyone else did, but I knew who was in control in the midst of the chaos. I walked in biblical hope, trusting that there was a future. I waited for change, with endurance, for solutions, with confident expectation in Jesus. I was grateful for all that governments, scientists, and health-care workers around the world were doing—for all that first responders and pastors were doing, and for all that neighbors and friends were doing for one another. But my hope, my confidence in the assurance of a future, was in Jesus. My hope was and is in Christ in me, because His presence in me is the assurance of a future glory, an eternal life beyond this earthly existence.

Let's not lose what we gained in that hard season. If our hope has shifted back to what we can do and what we have, let's recenter it in Jesus. Let's look to Christ in us, the hope of glory.

Jesus, I look to You. You are the hope that changes the world. You are the hope that changes my world. You are Christ in me, the hope of glory. Amen.

74 PUT HOPE IN
YOUR MAKER

*Happy is the one whose help is the God of Jacob, whose hope is in the L*ORD
his God, the Maker of heaven and earth, the sea and everything in them.
PSALM 146:5–6

Nooooo!" my oldest brother shouted as the winning numbers for the lottery were announced. "I played all my luckiest numbers! I hope and pray and think lots of happy thoughts! How am I not winning?"

There was no holding back when our entire family laughed hysterically at him. It was hard not to tease him for getting his hopes up so much when the odds were so stacked against him.

"Better luck next time, mate," my younger brother poked. "Looks like you're going to have to hold on to your day job a little longer."

As more of our family ribbed him, including his own kids, I couldn't help but think of how invested he was. He was so into it. How could he put his hopes in something that was such a long shot?

Of course, I've been just as guilty. I can remember being in high school and watching my favorite soccer team on TV. Wanting desperately for them to win, I ducked under the kitchen table and begged God to help them. Looking back, I wouldn't say that my petitions were biblical. I was sincere, sure, but I was definitely not putting my faith and hope in

God. I think I was more like my brother, hoping for the best; but not with the kind of hope that comes from God. I think it was more like positive thinking or wishful thinking, or maybe optimism. Those are all good, but they aren't the same as putting our hope in God.

When we put our hope in God, we're putting our confidence in God whose goodness and mercy are to be relied on and whose promises cannot fail.[39] When we put our hope in God, we're putting it in Jesus, the anchor for our souls.[40] What's more, when He died, the veil in the temple was torn in two.[41] We don't have to go through anyone to get to God. We can go straight to Him. We can go straight to the Source of all hope. Jesus is the anchor of our souls, and He is firmly and securely anchored behind the veil. He is the One who helps us endure.

Where have you placed your hope today? Let's remember to put our hope in Jesus and not in our optimal circumstances or the possibility of having a winning lottery draw. Let's put our hope in the One the psalmist called the Maker of heaven and earth.

Heavenly Father, all my hopes are in You, the One who made heaven and earth and all that it contains. In You, and You alone, is my confidence. In Jesus' name, amen.

75 SHIFTED AWAY

Now he has reconciled you by his physical body through his death, to present you holy, faultless, and blameless before him—if indeed you remain grounded and steadfast in the faith and are not shifted away from the hope of the gospel that you heard.

COLOSSIANS 1:22–23

Have you ever been completely caught off guard by something or someone—to the point even you were surprised how much it rattled you? How much it disappointed you? I have, and it's happened more than once. I have been shocked to realize at times I'd inadvertently put my hope in the most mundane things.

For example, when our girls were little, Nick and I had our air travel routine down. Once we got to a gate and checked in, he would juggle all the backpacks and I would run to get coffee for us. On one particular trip, after checking the time to be sure I could make it, Nick and I agreed he'd go ahead and board with the girls, and I would make the mandatory coffee run. I was so proud of myself when I made it back to the gate with time to spare. But when I started to pass from the terminal to the jet bridge, an airline employee stationed at the doorway stopped me and said I wasn't getting on the plane.

At first, I was confused. I sought to understand, and then I explained that my husband and children were already on the plane . . . and that the door to the plane was still open . . . and that from what I understood, it was well within the rules to let me board.

When she didn't budge, my confusion turned to shock, and then to disbelief, and then hot tears began to well up. I pleaded with her. How could she not let me on the plane? I wasn't late. I was the mother of small children. What about caffeine being a necessity did she not understand?

I'll never forget how I felt. Helpless. Upset. Hopeless. I understand that it was just about catching a plane, but that's the point. It was an everyday thing in my life, and there really was a span of time that I actually felt hopeless.

I eventually got on the plane, but why is it that everyday things can have the power to steal our God-given hope? To leave us in a panic? Or feeling so down?

If we are going to endure and finish strong in this life, then we will need hope and resilience, because our hopes will often get dashed. Everyday life will make sure of that.

What do you have planned for today? Whatever you have scheduled, put your hope in Jesus and not in your plans. Remain grounded and steadfast in faith, so you are not shifted away from your hope—Jesus.

Jesus, whatever goes my way or doesn't today, I endure because my hope is in You. In Your name, Amen.

PART 4

LOVE, HIS HEALING BALM

Without mountains, we might find ourselves relieved that we can avoid the pain of the ascent, but we will forever miss the thrill of the summit. And in such a terribly scandalous trade-off, it is the absence of pain that becomes the thief of life.

CRAIG D. LOUNSBROUGH

76 DO YOU WANT TO
GET WELL?

When Jesus saw him lying there and realized he had already been there a long time, he said to him, "Do you want to get well?"
JOHN 5:6

What a question! Here was a man who had lain beside the pool of Bethesda longer than Jesus had been alive, and Jesus asks, "Do you want to get well?" From what I've read in the New Testament, Jesus often asked questions, and always with a purpose, it seems.

In this case, what if Jesus was asking a far deeper question? What if He was asking the man if he wanted to be healed completely, and not just physically?

It's so easy for us to grow accustomed to our limitations, to the many ways we need healing spiritually, isn't it? To be defined by our wounds. To make allowances for them. To not really want to pay the price of change. He knows how easy it is for us to settle and live smaller lives than what He's called us to live.

I've felt Jesus ask me this same question before. Not aloud, but in my heart. And I knew it was because He wanted to heal me in my heart.

Isn't that what He does with all of us?

When we cry out wanting to be married, doesn't it stand to reason that His response might come with a question: *Are you ready for the vulnerability and transparency of being in a relationship?*

When we cry out wanting to move forward, doesn't it stand to reason that His response might come with a question: *Do you want to let go of the past, including forgiving all the people who have wounded you?*

Saying yes is definitely the way forward, but it means saying yes to so much more. When the man at the pool first answered, he told Jesus of his limitations, citing that he could never get to the pool in time . . . when tradition said that the angel stirred the water and then it would bring healing. Jesus ignored his answer and went on to tell him to get up and pick up his mat and walk. Jesus healed the man, despite his answer.

The name Bethesda literally means "House of Mercy" in Hebrew and "House of Grace" in Aramaic. When Jesus healed the man, He ministered to him both mercy and grace. When Jesus heals us, He extends the same mercy and the same grace.

Do you want to get well? Spiritually? Today? It's a question Jesus asks us over and over throughout our lives. He knows that the more we're healed, the more we will be able to endure. Let's answer Him the same way every time. With a resounding yes!

Jesus, yes, I want to get well. I want to be healed in every crevice of my heart, in every place where it's been broken. Thank You for Your healing power moving in me now. Amen.

77 RESUME YOUR JOURNEY

*The L*ORD *our God spoke to us at Horeb: "You have stayed at this mountain long enough. Resume your journey and go . . . to the land of the Canaanites and to Lebanon as far as the great river, the Euphrates River."*

DEUTERONOMY 1:6–7

C an you imagine what it must have been like for the Israelites to finally be set free from bondage in Egypt only to realize they were being chased by Pharaoh's army? And then to miraculously cross the Red Sea on dry ground and watch as the water swallowed the Egyptians' horses and chariots behind them? It's no wonder that by the time they made it to the mountain where God gave Moses the Ten Commandments, they were ready to stay put for a while. After all the harrowing adventure they experienced, I know I would have been inclined to pitch my tent and be perfectly content to never move again.

But there came a day when God said they had stayed at that mountain long enough. That it was time to resume their journey. It would have been so easy to settle where they were because they were no longer slaves in Egypt, but the best part of the journey was still ahead. The promised land was before them.

Have you ever felt so relieved to not be where you once were that you stopped pressing on to get to where God wants to ultimately take you? I know I have. There have been times I have come through something and settled in a place that was no longer the epicenter of my pain, but I still harbored the residue of offense, bitterness, unforgiveness, or hurt. I was happy to settle, but Jesus wants me to experience the freedom of healing in my spiritual promised land.

That's why He gently comes and whispers to each one of us, "You've stayed at this mountain long enough, and it is now time to embrace the fullness of your healing."

If that's where you find yourself today, it's the perfect day to resume your journey. Whatever it is that's caused you to camp for too long, take it to Jesus in prayer. Invite Him to heal your wounded heart. Whatever it is that He shows you, do it, so you can keep moving toward your promised land—that place where you will fulfill all that He's called you to do. That place where you will build more endurance for more of your journey.

Jesus, please come into my heart and heal what I can't seem to overcome. Show me how to do all that You prompt me to do. Help me resume my journey and fulfill all that You put me here on earth to do. In Your name, amen.

78 GOD LOVES YOU; GOD CHOSE YOU

"You did not choose me, but I chose you."

JOHN 15:16

hristine?" Mum asked. "Would you like to know the whole truth?" I had just reached for the baklava when Mum asked this all-telling question, and somehow, I knew. Searching her eyes for the answer, wanting it to be anything other than what I was thinking, I found myself saying it for her: "I was adopted too."

I was a grown, married, thirty-three-year-old woman, and I was learning for the first time that my eldest brother and I were adopted. That I wasn't who I thought I was. The funny thing is, of all the things that could have popped out of my mouth, I asked, "Am I still Greek?"

It was the comic relief we needed on one of the toughest days of our lives together. And what I said next astounded me even more, but it reflected the previous decade of my life—years in which I'd spent time learning the Word, giving all my heart to Jesus, and letting Him do one healing work after another.

"Before I was formed in my mother's womb—whosever womb that was—God knew me. He knit together my innermost parts and fashioned all of my days before there was even one of them. I am fearfully and wonderfully made. Even though I've only just found out I was adopted, God has always known, and He has always loved me. And since that hasn't changed, nothing has changed. I may not be who I thought I was, but I still am who He says I am. And I am more. I am loved. I am His."

My mum was as shocked as I was by what I said, but it was *the truth*. And it was the foundation of how I would move through the months ahead sorting out my heart, trying to comprehend what my parents had kept from me. That day, somewhere in the middle of all Mum said, she said the most beautiful words. Words that brought such healing: "I loved you before I knew you."

To this day, I cherish those words. They were the heart of a mother letting me know that she had longed for me and chosen me even before she laid eyes on me. When I think of those words, I can't help but hear the heart of my heavenly Father, the One who has always wanted me too. The One who chose me long before my mother did. The One who chose you, long before you ever chose Him.

Lean in to God's love today and let it wrap around you. Believing in His love is essential to enduring in our walk of faith on this earth. There is nothing that can separate you from Him and His love.

Heavenly Father, help it sink deep into my heart that You chose me. That You've loved me every single day of my life. Wrap Your love around me so I can feel it all day today. In Jesus' name, amen.

79 TAKE ANOTHER LAP

"March around the city with all the men of war, circling the city one time. Do this for six days. Have seven priests carry seven ram's-horn trumpets in front of the ark. But on the seventh day, march around the city seven times, while the priests blow the rams' horns."

JOSHUA 6:3–4

When I read the account of the children of Israel taking laps and marching seven days around the city of Jericho so the walls would fall, I see a nation of people building endurance. Growing in faith. Being prepared for what God had prepared for them. And I can't help but see my own journey.

In everything God has given me to do, I have had to take laps too. Not physical ones, but spiritual ones. I have had to take laps of faith. I've had to stand in faith, endure in faith, and wait for as long as it took until answers came. Until breakthroughs came. Until resources came. And with each lap I have grown in faith and endurance.

Isn't that what was happening with the children of Israel? God could have taken down that wall the first day they walked around it, on lap one. But He didn't. He could have taken down that wall on the second day, on lap two. He could have taken that wall down on the third day, on lap three. After all, He's God. But He didn't. It wasn't until the seventh day, when they had completed seven laps, that the wall finally fell down.

I wonder how exhausted and discouraged they felt. I wonder how many times they wanted to give up and tell Joshua that this plan was the most far-fetched yet. But they kept taking laps.

What are you waiting in faith for? What are you enduring in faith? Do like the children of Israel did. Do like I have in every endeavor God has called me to. Take another lap. It's the preparation process God has for you. He is preparing you for what He's prepared for you. There was so much ahead for the children of Israel. Yes, they had made it to the promised land, but Jericho was just the beginning of what they would have to face and defeat to possess all the land God had given them.

Could it be that's what He's doing in your life? Is He strengthening your faith, building your endurance, and doing all He can to ensure your success in the future? Don't quit now. Keep walking by faith. Keep taking laps. Because one day, someday, eventually, you will be on lap seven on the seventh day, and the walls will come falling down.

Heavenly Father, thank You for strengthening me. I will take another lap, and another, as many as it takes to be ready for all You have for me. Thank You for preparing me for what You have prepared for me. In Jesus' name, amen.

80 INVITE JESUS IN

The LORD is near the brokenhearted; he saves those crushed in spirit.

PSALM 34:18

Months after my mother passed away, as I found myself grieving and missing her, I unexpectedly found myself grieving my biological mother as well. She was someone I had never met and hadn't thought about in years. I remember being surprised that there could be this hidden tender place tucked away in my heart that I wasn't even aware of until the day I suddenly was. Until the day the Holy Spirit showed it to me.

It was so strange to think of her at that time. So unsettling. And yet I came to understand that it was the goodness of God, because He was clearly showing me that He wanted to bring more healing to my heart. It wasn't until He showed me that I was grieving the loss of two mothers, and not just one, that I even realized I needed more healing. I was so grateful to experience what the psalmist wrote about, that the Lord is near to the brokenhearted. That He does save those crushed in spirit. It meant so much to realize that God cared so deeply, that He was with me, and once again He wanted to do a work in me so He could keep doing works through me.

Maybe you've had surprises like this pop up in your own heart. It's so important not to ignore them but to take them to Jesus. From what I've experienced, our heart wounds—those unbearable aches that we often carry around, sometimes unaware—need just as much care and healing as our physical wounds do. And, as I found out, they can exist undetected for years. Whether they are the result of someone's careless words or thoughtless actions. Whether they stem from rejection, betrayal, slander, or abuse. Whether they were inflicted by a teacher, mentor, leader, friend, or spouse. Whether they seem embedded in our history and target us because of our ancestry, ethnicity, or skin color. If we don't take them to Jesus when the Holy Spirit shows them to us, they will eventually fester and seep.

Our wounds can seep as fear, insecurity, shame, bitterness, frustration, or anger. They can cause us to withhold love, mercy, grace, and forgiveness, even begrudging others.

When I found myself grieving both my mothers, I didn't want to ignore it. I didn't want to let it fester and affect everyone around me. I wanted to invite Jesus in to heal me more. I understood that the more we're healed, the more we can endure, strong in faith, strong in heart.

Has the Holy Spirit given you a glimpse of a hidden wound? Take it to Jesus. He is near to the brokenhearted. He saves those of us crushed in spirit. So, invite Him in.

Jesus, I invite You into my heart, into every hidden place. Please heal what's aching and broken. Please make me whole. In Your name, amen.

81 HOW GOD SEES US

So Naaman went down and dipped himself in the Jordan seven times, according to the command of the man of God. Then his skin was restored and became like the skin of a small boy, and he was clean.

2 KINGS 5:14

Long after I gave my life fully to Jesus, I began to risk my wounded heart by letting the people I loved come in a little closer. For years, to protect myself, I had kept everyone at arm's length. But when Nick entered my world, he was determined to get past all the blockades.

I remember one night in particular when we were dating, when he confronted me. He could feel my willingness at times to trust him, and he could feel the times when I would push him away. He knew that to go on with our relationship, something had to give. I did too, but trusting anyone frightened me more than anything else in my life back then.

After he confronted me on my back-and-forth ways, I finally broke and told him everything about my past and all the abuse I had suffered. It was the most vulnerable I had ever been in my life, and I had no idea if our relationship would survive such a tell-all. But Nick's response told me everything I would ever need to know about him. He pulled me close and wouldn't let go. He cared deeply for me, and he was willing to walk my journey of healing with me.

What has mattered so much to me through the years is Nick

understands that my healing, and yours, and his, and everyone's on the planet, is a process. Healing, for any of us, doesn't happen overnight. It's the Bible story of Naaman, a valiant Old Testament army commander who was stricken by leprosy, that speaks to this for me. Naaman sought a cure, and Elisha the prophet told him to dip himself seven times in the muddy Jordan River in order to be healed. He couldn't go to a prettier river with cleaner waters and just dip once. He had to get in the Jordan and bathe there again and again and again—seven times. I find this story a picture of how healing is such a messy process, but a choice Naaman had to make. A choice we all have to make. Especially if we are to endure this life of faith that we've given ourselves to.

If we trust God with our broken and wounded hearts, He will bring healing, restoration, and wholeness. It may take as long as seven times or longer, but He will do His work in us. He sees us beyond where we are, as who He created us to be. Clean and whole.

Heavenly Father, please help me be willing to endure the process of being made whole. I want to be healed in every part of my heart. Help me through the messy process. In Jesus' name, amen.

82 JESUS HEALS
EVERY WOUND

He heals the brokenhearted and bandages their wounds.
PSALM 147:3

One day, after flying headfirst over the handlebars of his mountain bike, Nick came hobbling in the front door with blood running down his leg. He had just begun to train for his first year riding in the Cape Epic in South Africa, when somewhere on his way to a near-perfect landing, he cut his leg—on the bike, a rock, we have no idea—and then he managed to make it back home.

After I helped him hobble to the kitchen island, we quickly assessed if we could clean it up and bandage it, or if we needed to limp back out to the car and head to urgent care. I totally can get nauseated at the sight of blood, but I did my best as we both took a look.

Deciding we could manage it, we cleaned it, put antibiotic ointment on it, and bandaged it well. Over the next couple of weeks, we tended to it multiple times a day. So many times when we were dressing it, I thought of all the different wounds we can endure, especially the ones to our hearts. Some are like scrapes or bumps that leave a faint bruise for a day or two. Like when we're not invited or included. When we're overlooked or dismissed. When we're misunderstood or misrepresented.

When someone is careless with their words, leaving us feeling angry or a little less-than.

I thought of the wounds that went deeper and took me a little longer to quit nursing them. Like the times I felt treated unjustly. When I was called names as a kid just because I am Greek and the daughter of immigrants. When I was treated differently just because I am a woman. When someone disqualified me because of my age when I was young, and later when I was older.

I also remember wounds that seemed so painful and so intense, I thought they would never heal, much like the gash on Nick's leg. Still, when I invited Jesus in to tend to them, to bandage them, just like we tended to and bandaged Nick's wound, they eventually healed. It's so much easier to endure in this life when we have a heart that's whole.

Do you have a heart wound that needs tending to today? That needs to be bandaged so it can heal? I have good news for you. Jesus heals the brokenhearted. He bandages our wounds. There isn't one He cannot heal.

Jesus, please tend to my wounds, the ones I know about and the ones I haven't begun to understand. Let Your tender mercy and never-failing love heal the places where I feel so brokenhearted. In Your name, amen.

83 A BIT MORE CLEARLY

He [Jesus] took the blind man by the hand . . . Spitting on his eyes and laying his hands on him, he asked him, "Do you see anything?" He [the man] looked up and said, "I see people—they look like trees walking."

MARK 8:23–24

Every time I read this story about Jesus spitting in the man's eyes, I have a visceral reaction. I am a germophobe and would have preferred He use some other method; but sometimes Jesus did things in strange ways, and this was one of those times. What's more, although Jesus did go on to heal the man, it didn't happen instantaneously like we might expect. From the story, it appears to be more of a process, because after Jesus spit in the man's eyes and laid hands on him, He asked the man, "Do you see anything?"

Why would Jesus ask such a question? Didn't He know if His miracle-working power was on point or not? I feel sure Jesus knew the answer to the question, but He asked anyway. When the man answered, he said he saw people, but they looked like trees walking. In other words, he saw, but not clearly. It was a tad blurry.

I can't help but think this is so much like us. Aren't there places in our lives where we are somewhere between blindness and sight? Somewhere between not healed and more healed—and we need to receive more of Jesus' healing grace? The good news for us all is wherever we are, Jesus doesn't leave us there, just like He didn't leave the man there. He monitors our progression. He tends to our wounds. And He invites us to receive more healing.

When the man answered that he couldn't see clearly, Jesus laid hands on his eyes once more, and his sight was restored. I find it so interesting that the man's healing wasn't immediate but more of a process. Isn't that how it often is with us? Sometimes what we need to be healed from is in a place that hurts more deeply than we can explain, and it can take time for us to be completely healed. I know from experience what a process healing in our hearts can be, and I know that Jesus can heal any wound.

Do you need more healing? When Jesus asked the man if he could see, the man in the story was honest. How freeing to know that it's okay to keep being honest about the hurt and the tension you feel in your heart until you are completely at peace and made whole.

Let's keep enduring in faith and inviting Jesus in to heal us. After all, like the man in the story, we can always stand to see a bit more clearly.

Jesus, thank You that Your desire to heal me never stops. Please keep coming in to all the places between where I am healed and where I need more healing. In Your name I pray, amen.

84 A HEALED HEART

"The mouth speaks from the overflow of the heart."
MATTHEW 12:34

Whom I was starting out in ministry, one of my mentors said, "Chris, never forget that the number of people God allows you to help is the same number of people you can hurt. Be wise and always treat people well."

When she said this, there was no such thing as the internet or social media. We wrote letters or sent faxes, so we could pause and think about what we were going to say. It gave us more time to be reflective rather than reactive. I remember taking the time to pray over my correspondence, over every word and sentence and paragraph and page. Today, with the speed of the internet, as soon as we think it, we can email it, text it, or post it from our phones. It's so much easier to post without thinking, and if we're not in a good mood, to post from our mood rather than from a place of love and grace and wisdom.

Despite what I learned from my mentor, on a few occasions, I've been guilty of sharing something on social media during a difficult season—when I've been hurt. Thankfully, I've had close friends who saw my posts and knew it was coming from a place of pain, and they called me. In love, they suggested I take down the posts, and I did. It's so important to have solid and faithful people in your life who love you enough to help protect you from yourself.

Because of my mistakes, I've learned to think and pray long and hard before I post anything, because I want to help people heal. I don't want to aggravate their already-painful wounds. What's more, I've learned to examine my heart, because that's where all the words and posts come from. Isn't that what Jesus said? Our mouths speak from the overflow of our hearts.

The way we ensure that we share words that heal and not hurt—including when we post on social media—is to keep inviting Jesus in to heal our hearts. That way, the overflow is words of life and grace and love and goodness.

What are your words doing today? Are they hurting or healing? Let's practice being more reflective than reactive, so when we're tempted to hurt instead of heal—when we're tempted to have a sharper tongue, to become negative or pass judgment, to post something that only serves to divide—we recognize it as evidence of our own hurting hearts. And let's invite Jesus in to heal us more, so we endure, speaking and spreading His love, encouragement, and kindness. So we endure, speaking His words of life and gentleness. So we endure, speaking from a healed heart.

Jesus, please heal all the places in my heart that make me hurt others rather than bring more healing to them. Help me be more thoughtful in all that I say and post. In Your name, amen.

85 HIS ENDURING LOVE

We have come to know and to believe the love that God has for us. God is love, and the one who remains in love remains in God, and God remains in him.

1 JOHN 4:16

A dear friend of mine has often said that what we don't deal with in one season will splash over into our next season. To me, that means any wounds we might have received in one season will follow us into the next if we don't find resolution. If we don't take those hurts and offenses to Jesus in prayer, forgiving those who have hurt us, and then inviting Jesus in to heal us, we'll take those hurts and every negative thing that goes with them from our old job into our new job . . . from our past friendship into our new friendship . . . from our last marriage into our new marriage.

I know how easy it is to make this mistake. When I was young in my ministry career, I was given a team of my own to lead. Because of the brokenness in my past, I felt immense pressure not to disappoint anyone. I first felt the need to prove myself to my leaders, to be worthy of their trust in me, to execute every task that had been assigned to me with excellence. Then, to my team, I felt the pressure to prove I was worthy to be their leader, to push them in the direction we all needed to go, to ensure we met our goals. But my sincere exuberance to lead well was overrun by my unhealthy desire for acceptance, and I pushed everyone too far. Because of the wounds in my own heart, I felt nothing was ever enough for myself, and I passed that on to my team. I didn't know how to endure the way God wants us to—with a healed and whole heart.

Once I realized this, I went to see a counselor and worked through that part of my woundedness. I apologized to my team, and their gracious forgiveness brought deeper healing to me. I learned a lot through that painful season and grew in my leadership capacity. I don't think I would be leading a global team today if I had not allowed the Holy Spirit to heal my deep wound back then.

What about you? Do you have wounds splashing over, spilling out to everyone around you? You're not alone. We all do it. But the good news is we can invite Jesus in to heal us every single time so we don't keep doing it. We can remain in Him and let His enduring love heal every corner of our hearts.

Heavenly Father, I trust You and I love You. I believe the love You have for me, and I invite You in to love me more. To tend to the wounds in my heart with Your faithful love. In Jesus' name, amen.

86 STRONGER THAN EVER

I will bring you health and will heal you of your wounds—this is the LORD's declaration.

JEREMIAH 30:17

While I was in Colorado, between Arrowhead and Beaver Creek, hiking my way through golden Aspens, I took it all in. The canopy was so breathtaking, the streaks of sunlight so bright, I couldn't stop thanking God. Remembering the most serious accident of my life on that very same mountain, I thanked Him for how strong both my knees were, something I once took for granted. It had been more than a decade since Nick and I had been skiing, when I told him to "eat my snow," and took off down the slope. No sooner had I mouthed off than I found myself in the middle of my second unplanned aerial somersault. In the air I heard the loudest *pop, pop, pop!* When I landed, I was in the most excruciating pain I had ever known, and within minutes I knew I was not going to be able to get up or get off the mountain on my own.

Ski patrol came to my rescue, loading me into a basket stretcher and pulling me down the mountain to a waiting ambulance. At the hospital, I learned that I had snapped my ACL, torn my MCL and my meniscus, and fractured my knee. There would be no quick recovery, and surgery would be required, because I would need a new ACL if I was to ever walk again. The day of my surgery, a physical therapist wasted no time in telling me how hard it would be: "The pain of the recovery is going to be far greater than the pain of the injury. The degree to which you are willing to embrace that pain is the degree to which you will find full function in your knee again."

It took months to walk without pain, without a brace, without help, but when I did, I walked with a new understanding: the degree to which I am willing to embrace the pain of recovery—including when it comes to the wounds I find in my heart—is the degree to which I will be fully healed.

As I kept hiking that day, I got to stand in the exact spot where I had landed, and I couldn't get over all that God had done in my knee—and in my heart. I had been made whole in so many ways. Spiritually. Physically. Emotionally. Mentally. There's such incredible perspective when we endure and make it to the other side of something, isn't there?

How has your heart been injured? Are you willing to embrace the pain of recovery so you can be healed fully? I promise you, once you are, and once the healing process begins, you will be stronger than ever.

Heavenly Father, thank You for Your faithfulness to me, that when I embrace the pain of recovery and the healing process begins, I will be stronger than ever. In Jesus' name, amen.

87 ALL IN

[Jesus] said to him, "Love the Lord your God with all your heart, with all your soul, and with all your mind."

MATTHEW 22:37

From the time my Sophia was a little girl, she always loved the theater and wanted to be an actor. She started acting classes when she was very young, and she signed up for every school and community play. Nick and I were convinced she was going to be an actor, until the year something changed.

Sophia had auditioned for the school play and gotten a role, but she was not as eager as she'd always been. She wasn't as excited or passionate, and after a few weeks of rehearsals, I asked her what was wrong. "I'm not sure, Mum. My heart is just not in it anymore."

What a telling statement. "My heart is just not in it anymore." Have you ever said that? About a job? About a dating relationship? About a hobby? Think about it: You can be in a marriage but your heart not be in it. You can be in a church and your heart not be in it. You can be at a job and your heart not be in it. You can be on a team and your heart not be in it. Sophia was in the play. She had a valuable part. But something changed, and though she was still in the play, her heart was no longer in it.

Have you ever been so all in with something but one day realized your heart just wasn't into it anymore? It happens to us all at one time or another, about important things and unimportant things alike. I'd venture it even happens to us about spiritual things.

Jesus told us to love the Lord our God with all our hearts, souls, and minds, but sometimes, without meaning to, it seems we become a little less on fire for God. A little less enthusiastic, committed, dedicated, obedient . . . because our hearts just aren't into it like they once were. It can happen so gradually. It can happen when it feels like our hearts have taken a beating. When times are difficult for a prolonged season. When something deeply disappoints. When life seems to overwhelm. And if we're not all in, it will be difficult to endure in faith the way we want.

When we realize our hearts aren't into Jesus and His Word like they once were, maybe it's time to do a heart check and realign ourselves with what Jesus said: "Love the Lord your God with all your heart, with all your soul, and with all your mind." When we love God with all our being, we're all in, and that's what we want, don't we?

Lord, help me align my heart with You today. I love You with all my heart, soul, and mind. I love You with all my being. I want to be all in. In Jesus' name, amen.

88 HE MAKES ME LIE DOWN

He lets me lie down in green pastures; he leads me beside quiet waters.
PSALM 23:2

God knows us better than we know ourselves, and He knows just what we need to replenish our souls so we can endure. He's faithful like that, and He knows that we need to lie down in green pastures from time to time—not literally, necessarily, but figuratively. He knows the perfect thing we need to do to rest—mentally, emotionally, physically, spiritually—and refuel.

I tend to be one of those people who can run at a million miles an hour, so I have to be intentional when it comes to slowing down and replenishing my soul. Over the years, I've grown pretty good at it, but it has definitely taken work. I've had to learn how to just sit in His presence. To be still with Him. I've also learned it's equally important to go for a walk or a run. To weave fun and adventure into my schedule and make time for people I care deeply about.

What is it for you?

When I don't pay attention to God's nudges to refuel, He gets a little more assertive in getting my attention. He might illuminate a Bible verse to me, or have a friend remind me to slow down, or He may just show me how tired I really am. I like how a few other translations of today's verse say that He *makes* us to lie down in green pastures.[42] Have you ever felt Him make you lie down?

When my girls were little, they ran around playing as hard and fast as I do in my work, so I had to make them take naps. I had to redirect their attention from running and jumping to slowing down so they could lie down for a rest. They totally fought it, of course, but every day, eventually, they gave up and fell asleep.

Doesn't God look out for us like we look out for our kids? I think so. In my mind, I see this picture of Him gently helping me to the ground saying, "Get down there, now," and though I'm sprawling in obedience, doing my best to relax, it's not always easy. It's not my nature to lie down in green pastures—and that's precisely why He wants me to do it. He knows I need to lie down in a pasture that will nourish me. In one that will give me great nutrition and vitamins and spiritual strength so I can go again. So I can endure.

If you're like me, and not too good at lying down, let Him lead you to some kind of pasture today. One that's green. One that's flourishing. One that will replenish your soul.

Heavenly Father, thank You for letting me lie down in green pastures. Lead me to exactly what that needs to be in my life today. In Jesus' name, amen.

89 PROTECT YOUR HEART

Guard your heart above all else, for it is the source of life.
PROVERBS 4:23

W hen Dawn first invited me to start climbing the mountains of Southern California, I thought of it as a physical challenge. As a way to spend time with her and other friends we invited from time to time. But it was what it did for my heart that turned out to be the most valuable. Being outdoors, seeing what only God could create, being in awe of His creatures—yes, even the bears and snakes and mountain lions I worked hard to avoid—renewed my heart in ways I didn't see coming.

The times we'd come out of a thicket after a long, hard climb, stand on a ledge overlooking a magnificent waterfall, and try to take it all in did more for me than I could understand at the moment. The smells of the forest; the fresh, clean air; even the changes in scents as we climbed, invigorated my senses. Reaching the summit and seeing other mountains we'd climbed, and the ones we'd yet to climb, inspired my faith. In a way, every step I took was as much a step toward the top as it was a step of faith, because every step took courage, strength, determination, discipline, and hope—all the same qualities required for our hearts to endure and to keep moving forward spiritually.

All of it helped me get a renewed perspective on how important my heart is. And how important it is to protect it, just like today's verse tells us to do. Guard your heart, it says; but to do so we have to get in touch with what gives us life and what drains us.

Hiking, I discovered, gives me life. The beauty I encounter replenishes me. It doesn't replace the spiritual activities that bring me life, like spending time in prayer and reading the Word and listening to worship music or going to church. But just like laughing with my girls or watching a movie with Nick, it refreshes me.

When it comes to guarding our hearts, let's ensure that we let things in that bring us life. It is as important as keeping things out that deplete us—the things that don't lead to a flourishing heart. I can get so caught up keeping negative things out that I can forget to fill my heart with goodness and beauty. Hiking has reawakened my wonder and has been good for my heart.

What about you? Have you identified what replenishes and what takes life from you on a daily basis? Take time today to do one thing that restores your heart, and then take steps to start guarding your heart above all else. After all, it is your source of life.

Heavenly Father, thank You for teaching me to guard my heart above all else. To guard my source of life. In Jesus' name, amen.

90 KEEP YOUR HEART

"Don't let your heart be troubled. Believe in God; believe also in me."
JOHN 14:1

At the entrance to so many trails in Southern California, there are signs warning hikers: "Beware of Rattlesnakes." Knowing how anxious I can get about them, Dawn would always hike ahead of me and prod her poles in the brush to ensure there were no snakes lurking on either side of the trail. She was so brave. But on one hike, a giant one outsmarted her—and it raced across the trail right in front of me. To this day, I'm not sure what happened when, but I saw a rattlesnake, pulled a calf muscle, and seriously wasn't sure I'd be able to get off the mountain.

I remember sitting down, nursing my leg, trying to get it to relax, to let go and let me walk, but it was locked up. Fellow hikers walking by encouraged me like everyone does on the trail, "You got this!" But deep down, I wasn't sure if I did. I remember trying so hard to concentrate, to not let my heart be troubled—which the snake had not helped at all—and to relax.

Seeing my struggle, a few other hikers passing by stopped to render aid. They were so kind, literally pulling supplies out of their packs to give me. Supplements. Energy bars. More hydration. They knew exactly what my calf muscle was doing, and they knew how to help. I took all their advice, and gradually, I felt it calming down.

Most importantly, I found my peace. I quit letting my heart be troubled. Can you believe Jesus told us to *not* let our hearts be troubled? The very idea suggests that we have control over what is going on in our hearts—even if there's a rattlesnake fraying our nerves. Basically, what I've come to understand is that Jesus was telling us not to let our hearts freak out, something I'm still working on.

I don't know what will come slithering across your path today, but make the choice right now to not let your heart be troubled. Remind yourself that you have authority over your heart. I know with all that goes on in this world, all the turbulent, chaotic, divisive, and fearful things we hear about and read about, it's easy to lose heart. But if we let the Enemy take our peace, he will get our heart. Isn't that what he tried to do to me on the mountain? When that snake crossed in front of me, I let it shake me up, and between it and my calf muscle cramping, I had to work to get my peace back.

Don't let your heart be troubled, so you can endure in peace. Believe in God. Believe in Jesus.

Heavenly Father, help me not let my heart be troubled today. Help me put my trust in You and walk in peace. I believe in You. In Jesus' name, amen.

91 SEE THEIR HEARTS

The LORD said to Samuel, "Do not look at his appearance or his stature because I have rejected him. Humans do not see what the LORD sees, for humans see what is visible, but the LORD sees the heart."

1 SAMUEL 16:7

When God wanted the prophet Samuel to anoint the future king of Israel, He sent him to Jesse the Bethlehemite, a man who had eight sons. As Samuel sought to anoint the next king, he thought surely Eliab was the one. He was tall, the eldest, and the most logical choice. He looked good and had a strong physique. But that's when God said to Samuel to not look at his appearance—that humans see what is visible, but the Lord sees the heart.

Here's a case where the prophet got it wrong. But don't we all from time to time? If Samuel had been picking the next king today, I wonder if he'd be scrolling through social media profiles, looking for the perfect person. Can you imagine trying to select someone from all the selfies filtered just perfectly? Or scoring each candidate based on the number of likes, shares, retweets, and comments?

It sounds funny, but isn't that what we do? Too often we look at who has the best body, clothes, and connections, when God wants us to look with His eyes, with His spiritual discernment. God looks through the filters and the edits and goes straight to the condition of our hearts, because the heart is everything to Him. Skills, talents, education, and experience are important, but not as important as our hearts when it comes to enduring in this earth and fulfilling all the purposes and plans God has for our lives.

How's your heart? A heart is proven over time. When it comes to protecting our hearts, I understand that we cannot control what life sends us, but we can control how we respond. To endure, to run our race on this earth and finish strong, we will have to take care of our hearts. We must choose to give the Enemy no ground because—make no mistake—the Enemy will try to take us out from the inside out. He will try to get us to be apathetic, or hardened, or legalistic. He wants us to have a spiritual heart attack. He wants us to quit. He wants us to be ineffective.

I want God to see my heart, and I want Him to like what He sees. I imagine you want the same. Let's invite Him in to heal our hearts, to strengthen them, to renew them, so we can endure and go the distance in this life. And when we look at others, let's see them through God's eyes. Let's see their hearts.

Heavenly Father, thank You for healing me and giving me eyes to see like You do. Help me look past people's appearances and see their hearts the way You do. In Jesus' name, amen.

92 AFTER GOD'S HEART

After removing [Saul], [God] raised up David as their king and testified about him, "I have found David the son of Jesse to be a man after my own heart, who will carry out all my will."

ACTS 13:22

Of all the qualities David possessed, the most powerful had to be that he had a heart after God. This does not mean that David was perfect, because we know from his failures that he was not. Luke does not say that David had a perfect heart, but he had a heart that ultimately was after God's own heart more than anything else.

Can you imagine being someone like David, and having a heartbeat that is so synchronized with God's heartbeat that His will becomes your will? That is the kind of Jesus follower I want to be. I want to be someone after God's own heart, don't you? Not my will. Not my plans. Not my desires. Just Yours, Lord.

I feel sure you know what this is like. Think back to when you were first in love or when you first became passionate about a new job, hobby, or sport, when no one had to make you do your work or practice your sport. You were all in. You went above and beyond. You came in early and stayed late if that's what it took. You had an "I want to" attitude, not an "I have to" attitude. No one had to talk you into anything. That job, that sport, that hobby had your heart, and that's how God wants to have your heart.

If our hearts aren't strong, I can't help but wonder—how can we stand up to all the pressure in this world and still have hearts after God? Think about it in light of our physical hearts. The heart muscles beating in our chests each have four chambers that pump blood throughout our bodies. The heart is always working, keeping us alive. It's the only muscle that never rests. The minute it stops beating, we are surely pronounced dead. We can live without a lot of things in this life, but we can't live without a heart.

Clearly, our hearts matter physically and spiritually. In the same way we need a physically strong heart to walk and live and run our race on this earth, we need a spiritually strong one too. We need to be like David, people after God's heart.

Have you checked your heart lately? If there's anything holding you back from being someone after God's own heart, then take it to Him in prayer today. Invite Him to heal your heart, to cover you with His love. Commit to being someone who will carry out His will.

Heavenly Father, thank You for transforming me from the inside out, that I would be someone after Your heart, someone who will carry out Your will. In Jesus' name, amen.

93 GOD'S WORD HEALS

Coasts and islands, listen to me; distant peoples, pay attention. The LORD called me before I was born. He named me while I was in my mother's womb.
ISAIAH 49:1

One of the most powerful moments in my life, when I felt God's Word rise up in my heart and do a work in me, happened about six months after I first learned that I was adopted. I was thirty-three at the time, married to Nick, and cooking dinner. I had requested my birth certificate and other related information months before, and it had finally come in the mail.

When I opened it, where my name was to be listed, it read number 2508 of 1966. There was no name. Just a number. Then, there was a social work report that essentially said my biological mother just wanted to get having me over and done with as soon as possible so she could return to work. I wasn't just unnamed; I was unwanted. From the start.

I remember sitting on the sofa crying, feeling like a knife had gone through my heart. Thoughts swirled in my head: *See, Christine. Your mother didn't want you. See, you were an accident. She didn't even give you a name. That's how little value you have. You are insignificant. You are just a number.*

It sounds so strange now, but what I did next was everything. I felt a prompting in my heart from the Holy Spirit to turn to Isaiah 49. This did not happen very often, but in my grief and desperation, I began to read today's verse, and I literally sobbed. I could not believe my own eyes. It was as though the words had been written just for me. And yet, in that moment, they had. Though my mother hadn't named me, my heavenly Father had. He had called me before I was even born. There I was, holding my birth certificate printed in black and white in one hand, and my Bible printed in black and white in the other. I had a choice to make. Which one would I believe? Which one would I let my heart embrace? I chose to put my trust and faith and hope in God and His Word.

I learned then that there comes a time in all our lives when we will be faced with the decision to believe what others have said about us, what we have said about ourselves, or what God has said in His Word. Only one will bring healing and wholeness to our hearts. Only one will enable us to endure and fulfill all the purposes God has for us. Lean in to His love and His Word today.

Heavenly Father, thank You for Your Word. Thank You for how it heals me and restores my heart so I can fulfill all that You've created me to be and called me to do. In Jesus' name, amen.

94 SANCTIFY US COMPLETELY

Now may the God of peace himself sanctify you completely. And may your whole spirit, soul, and body be kept sound and blameless at the coming of our Lord Jesus Christ.

1 THESSALONIANS 5:23

When I first surrendered my life to Jesus, I became an avid Bible reader and church attender. And because I was on earth when the dinosaurs were, I listened to additional sermons on cassette tapes. I wanted to learn everything I could, and I desperately needed help to change. I remember I often found myself able to apply the lessons I learned, and despite using all my willpower, I'd stay on track for about three days before I would start a downward cycle back into old patterns of thinking and behaving. Struggling to grow, I would wonder, *What's wrong with me?* and start to think that I wasn't spiritual enough. So I'd pray more, read the Bible more, fast more, and go to more church meetings.

Have you ever been there? It's like we think that if we just do more spiritual activity, we'll work out whatever is wrong with us. But that's not the answer. I stayed on this kind of treadmill for too long. I remember thinking, *I'm a loser. What could God do with me?* I desperately wanted to please the Lord. I wanted to live obediently, and I couldn't figure out why I just kept going back to my destructive ways.

What I didn't understand is that when I gave my life fully to Jesus, the Holy Spirit filled my spirit with His Spirit, but my soul remained the same. I had the same personality. The same habits. The same ways of thinking. The same approach to problems. The same ways of processing every negative thing anyone said to me or I said to myself. Nothing in my soul had changed. I came to Jesus broken and I was still broken.

It was just like my body. Whatever cellulite I had when I gave my life fully to Jesus was still there the minute after I was saved. Disappointing, I know! Nothing changed with my body or my soul. Just with my spirit. That's the part of me that got saved. But when I began to get teaching and understanding, and someone suggested I speak with a counselor, my mind began to be renewed and my soul began to heal. At the time, I was so full of unforgiveness, bitterness, shame, and anger, because I had not dealt with the trauma of abuse, abandonment, and rejection I had encountered as a child. But with help, I began to change. I began to overcome and learn how to endure in faith.

It's not enough to just give our lives to Jesus. If you came to Jesus with a wounded and broken soul like I did, or if you've been hurt since you came to Him, go to God today. Ask Him to heal every part of you, and that your whole spirit, soul, and body be kept sound and blameless.

Heavenly Father, thank You for saving me. Please continue to help me by showing me the places I need to be healed further. I want to be wholly Yours. In Jesus' name, amen.

95 HE'LL MAKE A WAY

"Look, I am about to do something new; even now it is coming. Do you not see it? Indeed, I will make a way in the wilderness, rivers in the desert."
ISAIAH 43:19

When my parents emigrated from Alexandria, Egypt, they came to Australia, and they brought all their Greek culture with them. If you could have come and visited our house when I was growing up, although we lived in Sydney in the 1970s and '80s, you would have thought we were living in Athens, Greece, in 1895. It's like they brought all our history and culture with them and we lived in a time warp. As my brothers and I grew up, we wanted to venture out. We wanted to experience everything that was new. But not Dad and Mum, nor our grandparents or any of our aunts and uncles.

I came to see that so many members of my family could have had so many more opportunities in Australia, but they chose to stay limited by the past and bound by tradition. And because of that, they missed so much of the future.

Can't we find ourselves doing the same spiritually? I think so. How many times have we stayed in something so familiar, so comfortable, so safe, all because deep down we were fearful of doing something new? I've been guilty of this, which is why today I tend to go full force into the new. I freely let go of anything that's not working, and I apply this principle to everything from workouts to how our team functions around the globe. In any area of my life, I don't ever want to get stuck in the past.

I have come to understand that if we are going to do all that God has called us to do, we have to be willing to not look back and hold on to past attachments. We have to be willing to let go of what used to bring us comfort, value, significance, or security. We have to trust God enough that we'll let go of anything holding us back from stepping into the fullness of what He has for us. That we'll let go of anything holding us back from enduring in faith.

Where are you today spiritually? If God is calling you to step forward into something new, you'll need to let go of the old. You might need to unplug from some commitments or some activities. You might need to shift some things from being a priority to being less important. No matter what, you will have to make room for the new thing God wants to do in your life and with your life. Are you ready?

Heavenly Father, thank You that I have a future filled with You. Thank You for making a way in the wilderness and rivers in the deserts in my life. In Jesus' name, amen.

96 HE'S GOT YOUR BACK

The angel of God, who was going in front of the Israelite forces, moved and went behind them. The pillar of cloud moved from in front of them and stood behind them.

EXODUS 14:19

About the time God told Moses to lift his staff and stretch his hand out over the Red Sea, so the water would part and the Israelites could cross on dry ground, the presence of God that had been going before them moved around to the back of them. The angel that had been leading them moved to the back as well. And the pillar of cloud moved too. God was about to do one of the greatest miracles in the Bible, but from the vantage point of the Israelites, it looked like He disappeared. Can't you hear them questioning God and asking one another, "Where did God go? Why did He leave us?"

It sounds funny, I know, but wouldn't it have been natural for them to question God because they couldn't see Him? Isn't that what we do when we don't see Him moving in our lives?

I know the times I've waited and waited on my prayers to be answered, I found myself asking God where He was. As if He'd disappeared.

I like it that God tells us in the story exactly where He went. He moved from in front of them to position Himself behind them. He put

Himself between the Israelites and the Egyptians, and the Bible goes on to tell us neither group came near the other all night long.

If you feel like God's gone missing today, consider that perhaps He's moved out of your line of sight, from in front of you, to position Himself behind you. Whether you can see Him or not, He's got your back. He's protecting you.

If you've invited Him in to heal you, or help you, or lead you, trust that He's at work, whether you see Him working or not. Knowing God is fighting battles for you in ways you can't see or imagine is one more way you can endure the challenges that come your way. Trust that God is keeping enemies away . . . trust that He's working things together for your good and His glory.[43] Sometimes I think we're waiting on a miracle when all the while a miracle is already taking place. We're waiting on the Red Sea to part, but God's already protecting us in ways we can't see or understand.

Whatever it is you've given to God, He is at work. He is a God of miracles and He's working on your behalf. It's hard to trust when you can't see, but that is when we choose to walk by faith and not by sight.

Heavenly Father, I'm so grateful You are always there, in front of me or beside me or behind me. Help me remember that You're at work in my life, especially in the ways I cannot see. In Jesus' name, amen.

97 CROSS THE ROAD

"He went over to him and bandaged his wounds, pouring on olive oil and wine. Then he put him on his own animal, brought him to an inn, and took care of him."

LUKE 10:34

When I first became aware of human trafficking, God used the Bible story of the good Samaritan to touch my heart and guide me into the future He had planned for me—the future of starting A21. I was preparing to speak at a conference using today's scripture when God emphasized a phrase that I'd never paid much attention to before: "He went over to him."

The more I studied, the more I couldn't stop reading that phrase. It's as though God wanted to prepare my heart as much as He wanted me to prepare a message for the people I would be speaking to. As I continued to seek Him, I found myself thinking about all the people in the world who are like that man lying on the side of the road. People who are heartbroken, abandoned, rejected, hungry, homeless, or tormented. And I couldn't help but think about the missing women and children I'd seen on posters in an airport—the people God would eventually send me and our team to reach, rescue, and restore through the work of A21.

At the time, I was a busy woman—a wife and a mother of two with plenty to do. I didn't need another venture; and yet it was clear God wanted to interrupt my plans for His purpose. God wanted me to cross the road for people I'd never met, never knew existed, and never knew were missing—the men, women, and children trapped in modern-day slavery.

Isn't that what the good Samaritan did? He crossed the road. He went out of his way, and he bandaged the man's wounds. Jesus had bandaged my wounds. He had healed me so I could endure in my life of faith, strong and hopeful. How could I not want to help bandage other people's wounds?

What about you? What wounds has Jesus bandaged for you? Perhaps there's someone He's now asking you to cross the road for. Perhaps He's shown you someone who needs to know His love. Don't miss an opportunity to metaphorically cross the street and be the hands and feet of Jesus to someone. A smile, a word of encouragement, a prayer, or meeting a practical need they have. People are waiting to be seen. To be known. To be loved. To be valued. To be helped. Crossing the street is what we are called to do as Jesus followers. We must roll up our sleeves and go to the trenches. A lost, broken, and hurting world awaits.

Jesus, I'm so grateful for the way You have bandaged the wounds in my heart. Please continue to bring healing into my life. And help me see who around me needs my help in bandaging their wounds. In Your name, amen.

98 STAY UNTIL YOU HEAL

After the entire nation had been circumcised, they stayed where they were in the camp until they recovered.

JOSHUA 5:8

There are a lot of reasons women can find to complain about being a woman—and granted, monthly cycles and the pain of childbearing might be two top picks—but today's verse always reminds me how glad I am not to be a man! Still, surprisingly, there's something in this verse for us all. When the Israelites left Egypt, they ceased to circumcise. An entire generation of men died off who were circumcised—and an entire generation grew up who were not circumcised. So, before they entered the promised land, the Lord told Joshua to circumcise all the men.

Here's why this is important: While we may not need to be circumcised physically, we will always need to be circumcised in our hearts.[44] There will always be things that need to be cut away in our lives so we can keep enduring and flourishing. It could be old ways of thinking and behaving; it could be friendships that are no longer life-giving; it could be attitudes of our hearts that are holding us back. It could even be things that are good. Sometimes, we need to cut away good things to make room for God things.

What I also find insightful is that after the men were circumcised, they stayed in the camp until they recovered, until they were healed.[45]

How important it is for us then, when we cut away something, that we give the corresponding place in our hearts time to heal. After all, it's a cut, and cuts are open wounds, even when they are good wounds.

Think about where you have been obedient to God to prune things from your life. Didn't it leave a sore spot? Perhaps when you walked away from a dating relationship you knew God wanted to end. Didn't it hurt? And yet you knew it was the right thing to do. That's one of those times we have to let our hearts heal before we move forward. If we move forward with a gaping wound, even from a cutting away we knew was right, we'll only wound others. Have you ever thought about healing from this perspective?

Wounds, whether they are from our past or from a cutting away, all need to be healed so we can endure and keep moving forward with a healed heart. Do you have a fresh wound? One that's good to have and yet still painful? Stay where you are camped out with the Lord until you heal. It's one more way you'll endure in the next place God takes you.

Heavenly Father, help me walk in this wisdom. To stay where I am, to spiritually camp with You, until I'm fully healed. Until I'm ready for the next adventure You've planned for me. In Jesus' name, amen.

99 SHARE YOUR FRAGRANCE

To God we are the fragrance of Christ among those who are being saved and among those who are perishing.
2 CORINTHIANS 2:15

One summer vacation, as I was searching for ways Sophia and I could spend time together, I discovered a perfumery that offered an afternoon of learning how to make fragrances. For four hours we were tutored by a chemical engineer who explained the mystery of how scents are a perfect blend of art and science—and how even one slight change in chemicals can completely alter a formula and the subsequent bouquet.

I learned that many perfumes are made by pressing and crushing flowers, fruits, grasses, spices, wood, and a myriad of other strong-smelling substances. The purpose of the pressing or crushing is to extract the natural oils. In ancient times, the oils were extracted, pressed, steamed, and then burned to scent the surrounding air. Today, the oils are extracted with much more modern methods, mixed with chemicals to enhance the smell, and then left to mature for a period of time before they are ready to be marketed. The creation of a scent is a lengthy process that involves multiple stages: compressing, crushing, steaming, boiling, mixing, and even curing for days, weeks, or months.

After the class, I couldn't help but think how the sweet fragrance of Christ comes forth as we endure the pressures of life and mature in our faith when we are tested, tried, and refined—when we discover places in our hearts that need to be healed and invite Jesus in. I could see how our untreated and unhealed wounds can conceal the sweet-smelling fragrance of Christ. But when we allow Jesus to heal us, we are able to express more compassion, more empathy, more patience, and more love to others. Isn't that what we all want? I think so.

Over the course of the more than thirty years I've walked with Jesus, the more healing I've embraced, the more fragrant the aroma I have exuded in my marriage, my mothering, and my ministry life. It's Christ in me that brings encouragement and hope to others.

I have found that it's easier to endure the painful process of healing when I understand that on the other side is a beautiful fragrance—one that positively influences the world.

What about you? Have you experienced the other side of healing? Did you find it to be worth all the pain? Especially when you saw how God could use it to influence others?

Remember this as you endure, and keep moving forward because there will always be more healing ahead. More fragrance to share.

Jesus, help me bring Your sweet-smelling and fragrant aroma to everyone I meet. Help me keep inviting You in to heal me, so I smell sweeter and sweeter. I love You. In Your name, amen.

100 THROUGH THE
BEAUTIFUL GATE

All the people saw him walking and praising God, and they recognized that
he was the one who used to sit and beg at the Beautiful Gate of the temple. So
they were filled with awe and astonishment at what had happened to him.
ACTS 3:9–10

I n the Bible story surrounding this verse—the one about the lame
man who sat at the gate called Beautiful and begged—the man asked
for money, but Peter offered him healing. The man wanted a short-term
solution and Peter offered him what he really needed—not pocket change
but a life change.

Isn't that like God? To take what is ugly and make it beautiful? To
reach out to us right where we are and heal us? To see beyond our crippled
brokenness to all the potential He placed inside us? To help us keep
enduring, to get to the next place in our lives, He offers us healing instead
of what we think it is that we need.

When I read this story in light of my own life, I can't help but think
of how we tend to overestimate what people can do for us and under-
estimate what God wants to do for us. God sees us beyond where we are;
He sees us as who He created us to be.

Peter told the lame man to get up and walk, and the man obeyed.

He made the effort to rise up. To move forward in faith. Isn't that all God ever asks us to do? God cherishes us in our brokenness, but He'll never leave us there. He sends people—like Peter and John—to notice us and show us His unconditional love. And then, as He heals us, He uses us to touch others, just like today's verse shows us. When the people saw the man walk through the Beautiful Gate and into the temple, they were filled with wonder and amazement. Soon, a crowd gathered, and it became the perfect opportunity for Peter to preach. The man was used as a witness unto the power and person of Jesus.[46] Can you see how our healing is always for more than just us? It's for all the people on the other side of our obedience. When the man was healed, multitudes came to Christ.

This is what He wants to do with us. He wants to lead us all through the gate called Beautiful, right into His presence. To put us on the path to our destiny, to fulfilling our calling, so multitudes can be helped. So let's keep enduring—together—for our sakes and for His. And for all the people He's called us to reach. Let's keep walking through the Beautiful Gate.

Heavenly Father, I want to walk through the Beautiful Gate in every area of my life and heart, so I can help others do the same. I entrust myself to You fully. In Jesus' name, amen.

NOTES

1. *Cambridge Dictionary*, s.v. "you've got this," accessed November 19, 2021, https://dictionary.cambridge.org/us/dictionary/english/you-you-ve-got-this.
2. International Olympic Committee, "'I Never Thought of Stopping': Marathon Man Akhwari on His Epic Effort at the '68 Games," October 20, 2020, https://olympics.com/ioc/news/-i-never-thought-of-stopping-marathon-man-akhwari-on-his-epic-effort-at-the-68-games/.
3. See 1 Corinthians 9:24–26; Philippians 2:16; Hebrews 12:1.
4. 2 Timothy 4:7.
5. Hebrews 10:36 ESV.
6. Dictionary.com, s.v. "endurance," accessed November 19, 2021, https://www.dictionary.com/browse/endurance.
7. *Vine's Expository Dictionary*, s.v. "hupomone" (Old Tappan, NJ: Fleming H. Revell, 1980).
8. ESV; KJV; NKJV.
9. *Merriam-Webster*, s.v. "endurance," accessed November 22, 2021, https://www.merriam-webster.com/dictionary/endurance.
10. "The Walls of Jericho," Israel-a-history-of.com, https://www.israel-a-history-of.com/walls-of-jericho.html.
11. "5467 Promises, Divine," in *Dictionary of Bible Themes,* Biblegateway.com, accessed November 22, 2021, https://www.biblegateway.com/resources/dictionary-of-bible-themes/5467-promises-divine.
12. Deuteronomy 31:6.
13. Hebrews 13:5–6.
14. Luke 4:18.
15. Romans 8:28.
16. John 3:16; Romans 10:13; 1 Peter 2:24; Psalm 34:17.
17. 1 Corinthians 13:13; Ephesians 2:8; Hebrews 6:19; 1 John 4:16.
18. Psalm 86:5; 1 John 1:9; 2 Corinthians 5:18–21; Psalm 23.
19. KJV.

20. "Habakkuk," in M. G. Easton, *Easton's Bible Dictionary*, 3rd ed. (Thomas Nelson, 1897), BibleStudyTools.com, https://www.biblestudytools.com/dictionary/habakkuk/.

21. Bryan Loritts, "Calling or Career?" CatalystLeader.com, May 29, 2019, https://catalystleader.com/read/calling-or-career; Genesis 2:15; 2:20. Some of today's devotion first appeared in *Undaunted* by Christine Caine.

22. Romans 1:17; 2 Corinthians 5:7; Galatians 3:11; Hebrews 10:38.

23. "The Marine Layer," National Weather Service, accessed November 23, 2021, https://www.weather.gov/jetstream/marine.

24. Hebrews 6:19.

25. NIV; ESV; NKJV.

26. Romans 8:28.

27. Luke 24:17.

28. Luke 24:18.

29. Luke 24:27.

30. Luke 24:31–33.

31. NIV; ESV.

32. "About the Race," Absa Cape Epic, accessed November 23, 2021, https://www.cape-epic.com/riders/new-riders/about-the-race.

33. AMP.

34. Numbers 14:30.

35. Numbers 13:27.

36. Numbers 13:30.

37. Numbers 13:33.

38. Numbers 14:24.

39. T. Prendergast, "Hope (NT)," in D. N. Freedman, ed., *The Anchor Yale Bible Dictionary*, vol. 3 (New York: Doubleday, 1992), 282–83.

40. Hebrews 6:19.

41. Matthew 27:50–51.

42. NIV; ESV; NRSV; NKJV.

43. Romans 8:28; Isaiah 43:7; Psalm 119:1–4.

44. Deuteronomy 30:6.

45. NIV; ESV; NKJV.

46. Acts 4:4.

ACKNOWLEDGMENTS

For any book, it takes a team to help an author birth a vision. I am so grateful to God for every person who brought their gifts, talents, and passion to this series.

To Elizabeth Prestwood: Having you alongside me as a collaborative writer made the writing journey as adventurous as all the trails combined. This is the seventh book project we have worked on, and there are many more to come. Forever grateful to and for you.

To Dawn Jackson: Thank you for asking me to go hiking. I had no idea what one *yes* would lead to, but I'm so glad for all the adventures that followed, and the ones still to come.

To our fellow hikers: You made our trips deep, meaningful, and more than hilarious. I love you all . . . Kate Czechowicz, Hilary Holmes, Evelyn Valenzuela, Amanda-Paige Whittington, and Whitney Wood.

To my family: Nick, it was you who ensured I had all the right equipment, who packed my daypack so many Saturdays, who willingly drove me to trailheads and back home when I wasn't sure I'd have the strength to do it. Thank you for believing in me. I love you. Catherine and Sophia, you are the joy of my life. Thank you for letting me tell so many of your adventures in this devotional. I love you both.

To Tim Paulson, MacKenzie Howard, Kristen Parrish, Mandy Mullinix Wilson, Sabryna Lugge, Kristen Golden, Stephanie Tresner, and the whole team at Thomas Nelson: Thank you for having such vision for these devotions. I saw one book and you saw three. You poured your heart and soul into every phase of this project. I am so grateful for this amazing team.

To Matt Yates: Thank you for your unending support and encouragement. You are a gift to Nick and me.

To Katie Strandlund-Francois: It was because of your commitment that every phase of this project stayed on track and got introduced to the world—timely, creatively, and descriptively. Thank you *@laurieanneart*. The artwork for the covers is stunning.

To our A21, Propel, ZOE Church, and Equip and Empower teams, volunteers, partners, and supporters: Serving Jesus alongside you in every corner of our world is the greatest privilege and honor of my life. Let's keep doing this.

To my Lord and Savior, Jesus Christ: You are the reason I will not only run my race but finish my course. You are so worthy of my all.

ABOUT THE AUTHOR

Christine Caine is an Australian born, Greek blooded, lover of Jesus, speaker, author, and activist. Together with her husband, Nick, she founded the anti-human trafficking organization, The A21 Campaign, a recipient of the Mother Teresa Memorial Award for their work combating human trafficking among refugees, and Propel Women. Christine and Nick live in Southern California with their daughters Catherine and Sophia.

UN
SHAKE
ABLE

365 DEVOTIONS FOR FINDING
UNWAVERING STRENGTH IN GOD'S WORD

CHRISTINE CAINE

ISBN: 978-0-310-09067-0

God is bigger than your current story. Bigger than fear or shame or that voice in your head that whispers that you are not enough, too broken, or too flawed. Join Him in a closer relationship—one rooted in truth and unshakeable. In this daily devotional Christine Caine encourages you to find confidence to live as the person God created you to be.

ZONDERVAN®

AVAILABLE IN PRINT,
E-BOOK, AND AUDIO

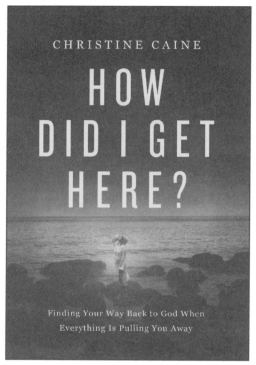

ISBN: 978-1-4002-2656-6

YOUR BEST DAYS ARE AHEAD OF YOU

It may not always seem like it, look like it, or feel like it—but it's true. In *How Did I Get Here?* Christine Caine invites us to press on—past our fears, past our mistakes, past our insecurities, past our comfort zones, past whatever is holding us back—to reach for more of Jesus and step into a life that is greater than we could ever hope, think, or imagine. Even when things are hard.

THOMAS NELSON
Since 1798

AVAILABLE IN PRINT, E-BOOK, AND AUDIO